LUNDY
SHIPWRECK and RESCUE

Robert Carl Smith

First published 2024

Old Light Press

© Robert Carl Smith 2024

No part of this publication may be reproduced, stored or transmitted in any form or by any means, without the prior written consent of the copyright owner.

ISBN 978-0-9541254-5-5

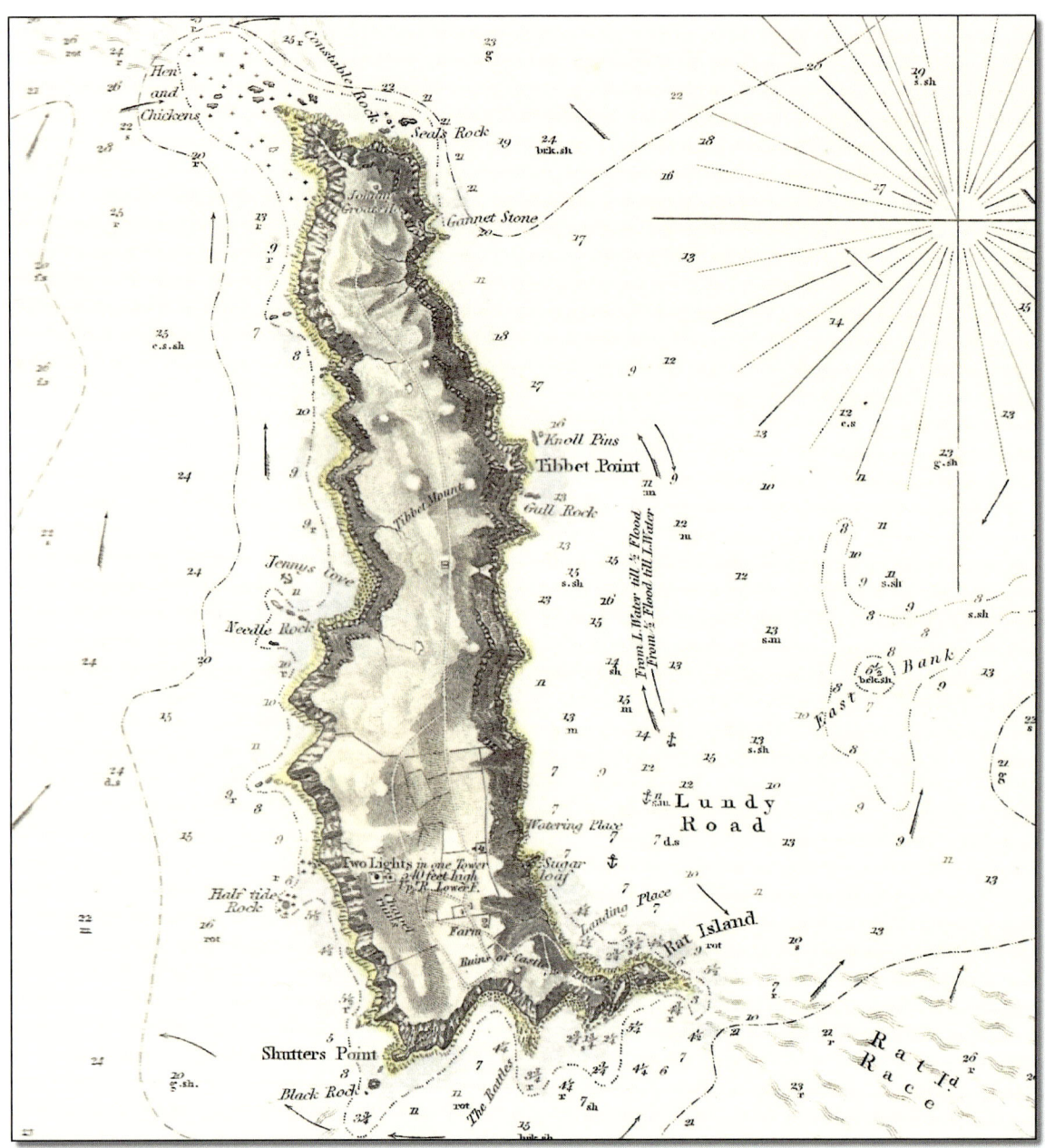

Lt H.M. Denham RN surveyed Lundy in 1832 and his chart was published in 1833

Contents

Map of South West England and South Wales showing Lundy and other places mentioned in the text 4
Introduction and acknowledgements 5
Map of Lundy showing places mentioned in the text 6
1732-1819: Coal, oranges and figs 7
Lundy's lighthouses 10
Vessels wrecked 1820-1839 13
Flag of distress 16
1840-1855: An apprentice the sole survivor 17
1855-1863: Emigrants for New York get no further than Lundy 21
The Shipwrecked Mariners' Society 25
1863-1865: No blockade running for *Iona* or *Matilda* 26
1865-1876: Nineteen drown on the *Hannah More* 30
"The Kingdom of Heaven" 40
1877-1883: SS *Ethel* wrecked on Lundy's Black Rock 41
1884-1885: A young lad the only survivor 46
1886-1888: The great gale of October 1886 48
1888-1896: Just one survivor of the *City of Exeter* 50
Bristol Channel pilots 56
1896-1897: Seventeen drown and two survive when the *Rajah* sinks 57
Ships lost 1898-1905 59
1906: HMS *Montagu* runs ashore 62
HMS *Montagu* – A tale of two shells … 64
Lundy's designated wrecks 65
1906-1914: Fog continues to be a menace 66
Rocket life saving apparatus 68
1915-1917: Seamen face another foe 69
1918-1939: U-boats sink hospital ships 71
The second world war to the 1990s 76
Bibliography and sources 80
Index of names of ships 81

South West England and South Wales showing Lundy and other places mentioned in the text. Adapted from Open Street Map © OpenStreetMap www.openstreetmap.org/copyright

Introduction and acknowledgements

MY INTEREST is not in the remains of ships which litter the seabed, but the circumstances of the loss and the battles their crews and passengers experienced in their attempt to survive. The following pages have many tales of death and destruction, lightened here and there by rescues carried out by fellow mariners and those who lived on the island of Lundy in the Bristol Channel.

The ships stranded, wrecked or sunk on or near Lundy were usually bound to or from Bristol or the ports of South Wales. The major industries involved were the import of African and West Indian goods, of copper and iron ores, or the export of coal and metal products. Some vessels were not bound to or from these ports but were driven into the Bristol Channel by severe westerly gales.

Earlier books and articles dealing with Lundy shipwrecks, which are listed in the Bibliography, contain many errors relating to the name, circumstance or date of a wreck. There has been a tendency for writers to copy mistakes without doing their own research. I have done my best to correct these errors by locating contemporary reports but, who knows, I may have introduced my own.

Though I studied maths and physics at university and worked as a school master I have always had a strong interest in the sea. Joining the crew of Mumbles lifeboat in 1967 prompted my interest in the history of shipwrecks and lifeboats. I began by reading the bound volumes of *The Cambrian* at Swansea Museum. The museum administrator, Betty Nelmes, was of great assistance to me and to all would-be historians. I am also most grateful to the staff at Cardiff Central Library and Bristol Central Library. Living in Surrey for twenty-five years I spent many Saturdays at London's Guildhall Library and the Caird Library of the National Maritime Museum, Greenwich, whose staff were of great assistance. I am also most grateful to Chris W. Dee for his photographs of the wreck of the *Kaaksburg*.

André Coutanche and Michael Williams of the Lundy Field Society added to my text to make it more accessible for the general reader. André did the design and layout and Michael's Old Light Press provided the imprint. I am also grateful to Chris Webster and Richard Breese for proof-reading. Richard also created the index of ship names.

Robert Carl Smith
Mumbles, Swansea 2024

Map of Lundy showing main features and other places mentioned in the text.
Adapted from Open Street Map © OpenStreetMap www.openstreetmap.org/copyright

6

1732-1819: Coal, oranges and figs

THE *Hopewell*, of Dublin, Captain Nicholas Dennis, sailed from Cork on 11 July 1732 in company with the snow *Fleece* (a snow was a square-rigged vessel with two masts with a third mast behind the main mast carrying a fore-and-aft sail). They were bound for Swansea to load coal for France. Late the next evening, when west of Lundy, they ran into a northerly gale and the *Hopewell* sprang a leak. The master of the *Fleece* saw she was in distress and stood by. Dennis, his three crew and a passenger, abandoned in the boat and rowed through mountainous seas to get to the *Fleece*. They had no sooner got aboard when they saw the *Hopewell* sink. Captain Dennis wept "There goes my all in the world".

The *Oliphant*, Dirk master, was bound from Dublin to Leghorn (Livorno, Italy) when driven into the Bristol Channel and wrecked on Lundy in the first week of November 1743.

Two vessels carrying coal from South Wales were wrecked on the island in November 1750 but their names were not recorded. Then in September 1757 the *Marie*, also with coal from South Wales, was wrecked on Lundy.

On 27 October 1758 the fleet under the command of Admiral Boscawen chased seven French men-of-war. The *Somerset* was able to seize the *Warwick* which had been captured by the French two years earlier. Night came on and the rest of the French vessels got away. One of these ships the *Hector*, of 64 guns, is said to have run ashore on Lundy.

When the *Chilgrove* arrived at Tenby from Poole her master, Turlington Cooke, reported that on 4 September 1768, when three leagues (nine nautical miles) north of Lundy, his crew had boarded an abandoned vessel. It was a brigantine or snow of about 140 tons named *Susanna*. The masts and bowsprit had gone and the deck and starboard side badly damaged. The vessel sank as the *Chilgrove*'s crew pulled away.

The *Nancy & Betsey*, Phillips master, was bound from St Ives to Swansea when she foundered off the island in February 1793.

In September 1794 the *Polly*, of Bude, Captain Bray, sank near Lundy drowning all hands. Then in the closing days of December 1796 the brig *Wye*, Captain Plaisted, of and from Chepstow with timber for Plymouth and Portsmouth dockyards was wrecked on the island drowning her crew.

The Bristol schooner *Jenny* was bound home from Africa with a cargo of ivory, dye wood and gold dust. The newspapers reported that "Having experienced for some days very foggy weather the ship's reckoning could not be accurately kept and in consequence she ran ashore and beat to pieces on the island of Lundy". Captain Buckle, his crew and passengers were drowned but the mate got ashore. The wreck occurred on or about 20 January 1797. The site of the loss, on the mid-section of the west coast of the island, is still known as Jenny's Cove. Sidenham Teast, the Bristol shipbuilder and trader in African goods, and his foreman John Gay, went to Lundy with the mate hoping to recover the cargo. A month later three French frigates and a lugger were anchored off the south coast of the island. They captured a timber hoy, removed her sails, and scuttled her (a hoy was a small sloop-rigged coasting ship or a heavy barge used for freight).

Bound from the Baltic to Dublin, the 119 ton brig *Myrtle Tree* was driven into the channel and wrecked on Lundy in the first week of January 1800. The 236 ton brig *Baltic*, of Yarmouth, Captain J. Sanford, bound from Newport for London with coal, foundered on 8 February 1809 off the island. In May 1809 the *Daniel*, of St Mary's, Isles of Scilly, foundered off Lundy drowning Captain Duff and all the crew. The *Concord* bound from Bristol for London was lost near Lundy in November 1810 her crew were able to row ashore.

The schooner *Estrella de Mar* was bound from St Ubes, Portugal, for Bristol when wrecked on Lundy early in December 1811. Her crew got ashore. Part of her cargo was salvaged and taken to Bristol where the brokers Lane, Edwards and Co. auctioned 121 boxes and chests of oranges and 200 frails of figs at their warehouse in St Stephen's Avenue on 23 December. Just in time to grace some Christmas tables!

> **FOR SALE BY AUCTION,**
> (For Account of the Underwriters,)
> On Monday next, the 23d December, at Twelve at Noon, at the Warehouse of the Brokers, St. Stephen's Avenue,
> ABOUT
> 121 BOXES and Chests ORANGES, 200. Frails FIGS, partly damaged, saved from the wreck of the *Estrella de Mar*, stranded at Lundy Island.
> To be put up in small lots, and viewed any time previous to the sale, on application to
> LANE, EDWARDS, & Co. Brokers.

Auction of the cargo of the *Estrella de Mar* (*Bristol Mirror* 21 December 1811)

In June 1816 the *Dove*, of Looe, Collins master, sank between Hartland Point and Lundy. The master's son was lost but Collins and the rest of the crew got aboard the boat and were saved. On Sunday 17 November 1816 the sloop *Rover*, of Teignmouth, Bartlett master, foundered between Hartland Point and Lundy when bound from Newport to London with coal. The crew were rescued and landed at Clovelly.

The 90 ton brig *Berwickshire Packet*, Captain Day, left Bristol on 24 January 1819 bound for Cork. She did not arrive and was believed to have sunk with all hands in a heavy gale which struck the channel. Lt Col Caesar Armett, of the 35th Regiment, and his wife Ann were aboard with their four children. The bodies of two of the children were found washed ashore on Lundy. Lt Col Carney, formerly of the 12th Regiment, was also aboard. A "foreign vessel" homeward bound from Liverpool sank near Lundy in the same gale drowning her master and five members of the crew; a ship sailing up channel rescued the eleven survivors and landed them at Mumbles.

> **BERWICKSHIRE PACKET.**
> ON board the Berwickshire Packet, which sailed from Bristol on the 24th January last, and is supposed to have foundered off Lundy Island during a gale of wind, was a Gentleman, LIEUT.-COL. CARNEY, late of his Majesty's service. As it is presumed, that the bodies of the sufferers have been, or may hereafter be, thrown on one of the shores of the Bristol Channel, the Friends of the Gentleman alluded to, desirous, if his body be found, to be immediately informed of the circumstance, are induced to resort to the medium of public advertisement to assure any person who may forward the particulars to Mr. JOHN CHEESE, Bookseller, Newport, Monmouthshire, that every expense will be paid, and the parties finding and taking charge of the body MOST HANDSOMELY REWARDED.
> The Gentleman supposed to be lost was 53 years of age, five feet nine inches in length, stout made, fair complexion, with a bold forehead, and had lost a tooth in front. In addition to the above description, the friends of the Colonel conceive it probable, that he might have had documents about his person at the time of the supposed catastrophe, by which his rank and name might be ascertained
> ☞ *This advertisement is particularly and respectfully addressed to the attention of Clergymen residing near the Coast, to Coroners, and to Custom and Excise-Officers generally.*

The *Berwickshire Packet* sank off Lundy (*The Cambrian* 6 March 1819)

The 73 ton sloop *Unity*, of Newport, Edwards master, was bound from Fowey to Llanelli with copper ore when she foundered north of Lundy on 23 April 1819. Her crew were rescued. The Swansea vessel *Vine*, Essery master, had a cargo of coal for one of the Cornish ports when she sprang a leak and foundered two leagues (six nautical miles) off Lundy on 14 June 1819. Her crew took to the boat and were picked up by the revenue cutter *Harpy* which landed them at Mumbles.

Some ship types mentioned in the text. Top left: Brig. Top right: Brigantine.
Bottom Left: Topsail Schooner. Bottom right: Lugger

Lundy's lighthouses

MERCHANTS AND SHIPOWNERS at Bristol and other channel ports had suggested the building of a lighthouse on Lundy from the early 1700s. Progress moved slowly so it was 1819 before Trinity House began work on the tower at Beacon Hill, the highest point of the island.

Trinity House – "The Master, Wardens and Assistants of the Guild, Fraternity or Brotherhood of the Most Glorious and Undivided Trinity and of Saint Clement in the Parish of Deptford Strond, in the County of Kent" – was established by Royal Charter in 1514 and is the General Lighthouse Authority for England and Wales (also covering the Channel Islands and Gibraltar). The Northern Lighthouse Board is the lighthouse authority in Scotland and the Isle of Man, and the Commissioners of Irish Lights cover the Republic of Ireland and Northern Ireland. Early lighthouses had been established informally by local initiative but in 1836 Trinity House were given compulsory powers to acquire and maintain private lighthouses.

When Trinity House arrived on Lundy, they did more than build a lighthouse. They improved the Beach Road from the Landing Bay to the plateau to ease the transportation of heavy goods. In the compound on Beacon Hill they built accommodation for two families of lighthouse keepers, joined to the tower by a corridor. In 1821, they built a house (now called Stoneycroft) for their Agent and for visitors. Later on, they built a separate house (since demolished) in the compound for the Principal Keeper when the staffing was increased to two Assistant Keepers. An outhouse was also built as a pigsty (now Old Light Cottage).

The architect for the lighthouse was Daniel Asher Alexander, who also built Dartmoor Prison.

(*Exeter Flying Post*
13 January 1820)

> TRINITY-HOUSE, LONDON, 23d Dec. 1819.
> *Navigation of the Bristol Channel.*
> **LUNDY ISLAND LIGHTS.**
>
> NOTICE is hereby given, that in compliance with the request of a numerous body of Merchants, Owners, and Masters of Ships, interested in the Navigation of the *Bristol Channel*, this Corporation have directed a LIGHT HOUSE TOWER to be ERECTED on the ISLAND of LUNDY, wherein Two distinct Lights, an Upper and a Lower Light will be exhibited for the benefit of navigation.
>
> *The uppermost Light* will revolve in an Horizontal Row, without any interval of Darkness, illuminating the whole Circle of the Horizon.
>
> *The lower Light*, placed 30 feet below the upper, will shew a fixed and steady light, extending over 90 degrees of the Horizon only, or from N. N. W. to W. S. W. by Compass.
>
> By which arrangement all Vessels entering the Bristol Channel will be enabled readily to distinguish the Lights on the Island of Lundy from all others in that vicinity.
>
> The necessary works for the exhibition of the aforesaid Lights are proceeding with all possible dispatch, and are expected to be complete in about Two Months from the date hereof.
>
> Farther notice will be published when the Lights are ready to be exhibited.

Marker stone erected by Trinity House on the Beach Road

The light built on Beacon Hill

The work is solid and elegant – but it was built in the wrong place. There is often low cloud and fog which obscures the light while the ground is clear. As a result, in 1862, Trinity House built "The Battery", a fog signal station, on the west coast half-way down the cliff. The fog warning was supplied by two cannon, firing blanks, and two gunners and their families were accommodated in a pair of substantial semi-detached cottages.

The crews of vessels which ran ashore on the island in fog often stated that they had been unable to see the light or even hear the fog signal. The fog cannon were replaced by rockets in 1878.

The *Shipping and Mercantile Gazette* of 9 February 1883 carried a letter from John C. Dennis, harbour master at Ilfracombe, in which he said that vessels were often wrecked on Lundy because the light had been placed so high as to be practically useless in fog. He suggested that Trinity House should be asked to place two lights on the island, one on or near Rat Island and the other at the north end as low as possible.

> **NOTICE TO MARINERS.**
>
> BRISTOL CHANNEL.
>
> TRINITY HOUSE, London, 26th June, 1878.
>
> FOG SIGNAL at LUNDY ISLAND.—Notice is hereby given, that on and after 1st August next, Rockets, specially prepared for the production of Sound, will be substituted for the Gun, as the Fog Signal at Lundy Island.
> During fog, and in thick weather, a Rocket (which on reaching an altitude of about 600 feet will explode with a loud report), will be discharged every 10 minutes.
> By order, ROBIN ALLEN, Secretary.

(*Lloyd's List* 26 June 1878)

In November 1888 Dennis once again suggested that the light at Beacon Hill should be replaced by two lights – one on the north end of the island and the other at the south – as low down and as far out as practicable. Trinity House took some time to act so it was not until 1897 that the new lights were lit.

The South Light from the Castle, also showing Rat and Mouse Islands and the jetty built in 1999

The North Light

Trinity House Notice to Mariners with details of the new lights (*The Standard* 22 November 1897)

```
NOTICE TO MARINERS.—(No. 20).—WEST
    COAST OF ENGLAND.—BRISTOL CHANNEL—
LUNDY ISLAND LIGHTS AND FOG SIGNALS. (All
Bearings are Magnetic).
        TRINITY HOUSE, LONDON, 19th November, 1897.
  In accordance with Notice to Mariners No. 7 dated 21st May,
1897, Lights of the following description are now exhibited
from Sunset to Sunrise, from the New Light Houses at the
North and South ends of Lundy Island, and a Fog Signal of
the character given below has been established at each Light
House.
                    NORTH LUNDY.
  The Light House, which is circular in shape and white in
colour, is about 56 feet in height from base to vane. It stands
at the extreme N.N.W. end of the Island, in a position N. 15°
E, 2 miles ⅔rds cable from the old Light House.
  The focal plane of the Light is 165 feet above High Water
Spring Tides. The Light gives two White Flashes in quick
succession every 20 Seconds, viz.:—Flash ⅔rds Second, short in-
terval 2 Seconds, Flash ⅔rds Second, long interval 15⅔rds
Seconds, and is visible for a distance of 19 miles in clear
weather, between the bearings of S. 28° W., through W. and N.
to S. 56° E.
                           |  Clear    |  Thick
                           | Weather.  | Weather.
                           +-----------+-----------
The intensity of the Light is equal to | Candles | Candles
                           |  81,000   | 121,500
  The Fog Signal is a Siren, which in thick or foggy weather
gives 4 Blasts Low, High, Low, High, of 2 Seconds duration
each, with short intervals of 2 Seconds between them, every
Two Minutes.
                    SOUTH LUNDY.
  The Light House, which is circular in shape and white in
colour, is about 52 feet in height from base to vane. It stands
at the S.E. point of the Island, in a position S. 45° E., 7 2-5ths
cables from the old Light House.
  The focal plane of the Light is 175 feet above High Water
Spring Tides. The Light is White, revolving every Minute,
and is visible for a distance of 20 miles in clear weather,
between the bearings of N. 10° E., through E. and S. to N.
89° W.
                           |  Clear    |  Thick
                           | Weather.  | Weather.
                           +-----------+-----------
The intensity of the Light is equal to | Candles | Candles
                           |  40,000   |  60,000.
  The Fog Signal is an Explosive, which gives one report in
thick or foggy weather every 10 Minutes.

  The High and Low Lights exhibited from the Tower
hitherto in use, have been discontinued, as well as the Rocket
Fog Signal.
  The old Light House Tower will be maintained as a Sea
Mark.         By Order.
                    CHAS. A. KENT, Secretary.
```

The construction of the South and North Lights also resulted in Trinity House upgrading Lundy's main north-south track which connected the two. Large stone blocks were placed the length of the track to mark its route in snow or poor visibility. A tradition persists that the blocks were specified to be one cubic foot in size but the plans were misread to say one cubic yard. A telephone line was installed to connect the two lights and the remains of telephone poles can be found in places near the main track.

The replacement of the original lighthouse on Beacon Hill by the South and North Lights resulted in what then became known as the "Old Light" reverting to the owner of the island. The keepers' accommodation is now letting cottages and the tower is open to all. The view from the lantern is spectacular.

All Trinity House lighthouses have been de-manned. Lundy North Light was automated in 1985 and became the first Trinity House lighthouse to be converted to solar powered operation in 1991. Lundy South Light was automated and converted to solar power in 1994. Both Lundy lights are now monitored and controlled from Trinity House's Planning Centre in Harwich, Essex. The traditional "fog horns" have also been removed. Similarly, the lightships referred to in this book have been withdrawn and converted to automatic buoys.

Vessels wrecked 1820-1839

ON THE EVENING of 20 January 1820 a vessel was wrecked on the island. The following day three bodies were found, along with an oar marked *Lamb*. The vessel may have been the 58 ton sloop *Lamb*, of Bideford. The sloop *Thomas & Ann*, Acard master, was bound from Carmarthen for Bristol with a cargo of oats. Good progress had been made but the south-west wind then backed to east and blew a full gale. The sloop was driven down channel and sank between Hartland and Lundy on 16 December 1820. Her crew took to the boat and reached the island.

The *Fame*, Gilmore master, was bound from Bristol for Cork when she missed stays (failed to change tack) and was wrecked on the rocks on Lundy's east coast on 7 February 1822. Her crew got ashore and a considerable part of the cargo, which included leather goods, glass and iron, was salvaged and returned to Bristol. Later that month a foreign vessel sank off the island, her topmasts being visible at low water.

> *For Account of the Underwriters.*
>
> To IRONMONGERS, SMITHS, &c.
> TO BE SOLD BY AUCTION,
> By WILLIAM JORDAN,
> At the IRON WAREHOUSE of Mr. JOHN WEBB, MARSH-STREET, Bristol, on TUESDAY NEXT, the 11th of April,
>
> TEN TONS of Damaged IRON NAIL RODS, being a part of the CARGO saved from the Wreck of the *Fame*, Capt. Gilmore, lost on Lady Island. It will be put up in Lots of Five Hundred Weight each, and will be sold without reserve, as it is for the benefit of te Underwriters.
> The Sale to commence at Eleven o'Clock.

Auction of the cargo of the *Fame* (*Bristol Mirror* 6 April 1822)

The 204 ton brig *Morrison*, of Kinsale, Captain John Dunbar, left Cork on Tuesday 28 October 1823 bound for Newport with nine crew, nineteen passengers and over two hundred pigs. With the west wind they made good progress up channel. At ten on Wednesday evening they saw the light on Flat Holm but the wind had veered to north-east and snow began to fall. On Thursday a violent gale drove them back down channel. At 3 pm they could just make out Nash Point as they were driven further west as the wind rose to storm force. The ballast shifted and the pigs ran to one side of the deck. The vessel was now almost on her beam ends. Repeated attempts were made to wear ship (turn away from the wind) but being waterlogged she struck the east coast of Lundy at about 10 pm and was dashed to pieces on the rocks. The master, one seaman and the boy clung to a mast and survived. Another man reached the rocks but died during the night in the severe cold. Five of the crew and all the passengers drowned.

The Sunderland brig *Comus*, Laws master, was bound from Jersey for Swansea when she ran ashore on the west coast of Lundy in thick weather on the night of Thursday 14 April 1825. Her master and crew of eight got ashore. The 153 ton vessel was wrecked but her masts, rigging and materials were salvaged. A Pill pilot cutter, Dignis master, landed the crew at Ilfracombe.

Bound from Penzance to Swansea with copper ore, the 60 ton sloop *Venus*, of Bridport, foundered off Lundy on Friday 1 December 1826, drowning seaman Doble. Captain Andrews and the remaining members of the crew were picked up.

On the morning of 22 April 1827 the brigantine *I.O.*, of and from Jersey for Cardiff, Captain le Gallais, was struck by a brig near Lundy. The brigantine filled and one of her crew was drowned. The brig sailed on and gave no assistance to the survivors who clung to the wreck for six hours until rescued by the *Ann & Mary*, Captain Cornish, which landed them at Padstow. The *I.O.* drifted ashore at South Hole, to the south of Hartland Point, two days later where she broke up after some of her materials had been salvaged.

The schooner *Speculation*, of St Ives, Bryant master, had taken a cargo of copper ore to Llanelli and was returning to Hayle with coal. A gale was blowing and at 2 am on 14 February 1828 a topping-lift parted and the boom fell onto one of the pumps with such force that a plank was loosened in the hull. The sea rushed in and the master and one seaman were able to launch the boat but two others went down as the vessel sank to the west of Lundy. The plug was out of the boat's hull and they had to take turns to push a finger into the hole. After sculling with one oar for ten hours Bryant and the seaman were rescued by a Bristol pilot skiff.

The vessel *Jeune Emma*, of Cherbourg, has been mentioned in some books relating to Lundy. She was bound from Martinique to Le Havre and on the evening of 20 November 1828 her master saw a light, possibly that on Lundy, which he believed was that at Ushant (west of Brittany). Sailing north the ship was wrecked on the Cefn Sidan (Silken Ridge) in Carmarthen Bay. Six members of the crew survived but the master, six men and six passengers drowned. One of the passengers was twelve-year-old Adeline, a niece of Josephine de Beauharnais, one-time wife of Napoleon Bonaparte.

The 98 ton brig *Hope* was owned by the Bridgwater and Taunton Shipping Company and was a regular trader to London. Bound home with a cargo of wheat and deals on the morning of 28 April 1829 she "rounded the land" between six and seven o'clock in good weather. The wind freshened from the south-west and in the afternoon Captain William Edwards got the crew to shorten sail. A nasty cross sea was making progress difficult but by 5 pm they were to the south of Lundy. Then the wind backed to the east and blew a gale. Edwards got the crew to pump the vessel and to heave the deck cargo of deals over the lee side. A heavy sea struck the brig throwing Loveless, one of the boys, overboard where he drowned. The *Hope* was now on her broadside and the yards struck the sea. The crew, except for the boy Trood who was in the cabin, got onto the vessel's side and clung to the chain bolts. They hailed a skiff a little ahead of them and it put about to make for the brig. The *Hope* capsized throwing Edwards and his crew into the sea where they each got hold of a deal. Two men were close to the stern and drawn down as the brig sank. Edwards got hold of a group of deals and was able to climb onto them. The mate was near him and holding onto one. The skiff arrived and its crew threw Edwards a rope and got him aboard. A rope was then thrown to the mate, and he caught it, but being very weak put it in his mouth to hold it with his teeth. He failed and sank. Edwards had been in the water for an hour. The skiff landed him at Clovelly on the afternoon of the 29th. Later that day he wrote to the owners to inform them of the loss of their vessel and crew.

The *Devonport Telegraph* reported in March 1829 that the *Frances Anne*, which had arrived at Portreath from Swansea, had struck a sunken rock three cables (about 600 yards) south by west from the east end of Rat Island. As the rock was not on the charts the item was entitled "Caution to Mariners".

The sloop *Unity*, of Barnstaple, Robert Yeo master, was bound home from Burry Port, Carmarthenshire, when she sprang a leak and foundered a few miles west of Lundy on 12 January 1833. The vessel sank so quickly that Yeo had no time to save his watch and money. He and the crew launched the boat and got safely to Clovelly. The press reported that a subscription had been opened to support Yeo "who is a worthy and enterprising young man".

Some writers have the steam packet *Erin* listed as a Lundy wreck. In the gale of 21 January 1833 she was seen in distress at least forty miles to the west of the island. The gale was so severe that passing vessels were unable to assist. Where she went down is not known but a trunk belonging to her master was found in St Bride's Bay on the Pembrokeshire coast. She had a crew of twenty-five and carried about thirty passengers from London and Plymouth bound for Dublin and Belfast.

The 153 ton schooner *Rapid*, of Sunderland, Colling master, Llanelli to London with coal, foundered near Lundy on 21 August 1835. Her crew got ashore. An abandoned brig was found five miles to the east of Lundy on 18 March 1836. It was lying on its port side with part of the starboard side above water. Parts of the rigging were landed at Ilfracombe but the name of the vessel and what became of the crew seems not to have been reported. The 48 ton sloop *Robert & Mary*, of Brixham, with coal from Swansea for Barnstaple, sank off Lundy on 2 April 1836.

The barque *Abbotsford*, Hicks master, was bound from Bristol to Boston, U.S.A., when she struck a rock on the east side of Lundy at 3 am on 6 April 1836. She was in contact with the rock for just a quarter of an hour but was leaking and sailed for Ilfracombe straight away having lost her fore-foot and jib-boom. After temporary repairs there she returned to Bristol where her cargo was discharged and she underwent a full repair.

The *Ostendais*, Captain Delperrie, was bound for Ostend from Liverpool and abandoned in a sinking condition to the south-west of Lundy at 10 pm on 18 September 1836. The master reported that his vessel had eight or nine feet of water in the hold and he could see no possibility of saving her. The crew of six pulled ashore at St Ives at ten the next morning. A couple of weeks later a table was washed up near Bideford containing the vessel's logbook.

The *Exeter and Plymouth Gazette* of 12 November 1836 carried a letter from Lundy. It said that on Saturday 8 October a boat was seen coming up from the south-west. The lighthouse keeper, James Cornish, was asked to go to wave its crew round to the landing place. Malbon, steward to Lundy's owner, William Heaven, launched his boat and rounded Surf Point to meet them. He towed them ashore and got them up to the house. They changed into dry clothes and were made comfortable. They were the crew of the Danish schooner *Faders Minde*, Captain J.C. Kjarit, which had left Newport with iron for Antwerp. The vessel ran into a gale ten leagues (30 nautical miles) to the west of Lundy and was so disabled that the crew of seven had to abandon. They left her at 7 am on Friday 7 October in the long boat taking food and essentials with them but had left only a short time when the seas stove in the boat. They got back aboard the schooner and launched the jolly boat which was just ten feet long. They were all exhausted and one man was so weak that he could not walk without assistance. The Danes left the next day aboard Bristol pilot cutter No. 1 and were taken up to Pill.

The brig *Elizabeth & Ann*, of Sunderland, left Newport for Bathurst, New Brunswick, in ballast on Sunday 20 August 1837. Four days later she anchored in Lundy roads to shelter from a near gale from the south-west. The wind then backed to the east and she was struck by a barque and schooner which were also sheltering there. The brig drove ashore and became a wreck. Captain Askey and his crew were rescued and landed at Bideford by a fishing smack.

The schooner *Elizabeth*, of Llanelli, was abandoned in a sinking condition on 13 March 1838. Her crew took to the boat and drifted up channel for two days eventually getting ashore near Nash Point lights on the Glamorgan coast from where they set out for home. The *Elizabeth* ran ashore on Lundy. A day later the vessel floated at high water with a piece of rock through the hull and was towed by the schooner *Ann*, Captain Tatem, to Appledore.

The schooner *Pilot*, of Llanelli, 270 tons burthen, T. Griffiths master, was a regular trader to the Cornish ports. She sailed from Hayle on 16 March 1838 bound for Llanelli to load a cargo of coal. A heavy gale struck that day and she was seen between Lundy and Caldy Island by the brig *Riviere* which soon lost sight of her. The *Pilot* did not arrive at Llanelli and her owners appealed through the *Shipping and Mercantile Gazette* for any news.

With a cargo of culm (small coal) from Neath the sloop *Unity*, of Salcombe, George Dornom master, was bound home. On the evening of 11 November 1838 she was run down about ten miles west of Lundy by the schooner *Quicksilver*, of Fowey. The sloop sank so quickly that the boy, who was in the forecastle, had no chance of escaping and his shrieks were clearly heard as the vessel went down. The master and mate were picked up by the schooner.

Sections of a wreck were reported a few miles to the north-east of Lundy on 14 December 1838. This was probably the remains of the *John & Mary*, of Sunderland, which had sailed from Miramichi, New Brunswick, Canada, on 1 November with timber for Stockton-on-Tees. The vessel had lost her masts and was waterlogged by a storm which swept four of her crew overboard. The vessel drifted into the Bristol Channel where the eight survivors were rescued by the *Kingston*, Captain Key, bound for Bristol from Quebec. When the survivors landed they were taken straight to Bristol Infirmary.

Flag of distress

THE RED ENSIGN *(left)* has been flown in its current form by British-registered merchant ships since 1801. The top quarter of the flag nearest the flagpole shows the Union Flag or Union Jack, the national flag of the United Kingdom.

Unlike the ensigns of many other countries, therefore, the British Red Ensign can be flown upside down.

For many years before other distress signals were standardised, hoisting the Red Ensign upside down *(right)* was a common way for a ship to indicate that it was in distress and that aid was requested. This was known as flying the ensign "union down" or "jack down".

1840-1855: An apprentice the sole survivor

THE brig *Woodman*, of and for Yarmouth from Swansea with 160 tons of stone coal, sank on 22 July 1840 eight miles east-north-east of Lundy after colliding with the *Neptune*, of Exeter. The *Neptune* picked up the *Woodman*'s crew, who had been unable to save anything, and landed them at Neath.

The brig *Rochdale*, of Whitehaven, William Kewley master, was bound from Barrow to Cardiff with iron ore when found to be leaking nine miles north-west of Lundy on 5 August 1840. The crew hoisted the ensign "union down" and took to the boat at 2.30 pm as they saw a vessel approaching. They were taken aboard the schooner *Gower*, of St Ives, Captain Hodge, which stood by until the brig sank at 4 pm. The crew, who lost their clothes, and Kewley, his charts and quadrant, were landed at Llanelli the next day.

A strong north-west gale was blowing on 14 November 1840 when many vessels arrived at Mumbles roads for shelter. Among them was the smack *Four Friends*, of Looe, Captain Scantlebury, which had been bound from Glasgow to Southampton and had been driven up channel by the gale which had first blown from south-west. When seven miles west by north of Lundy at 8 am on the 13th her crew had seen a brig sink. They found apprentice John Winchester, a native of Shetland, on a deck plank and picked him up. The brig was the *Alert*, which had sailed from Hayle with a cargo of copper ore and "mundic" (iron pyrites) for North Shields on the 12th. The rest of the crew had drowned – they were John Gregson, the master, of Sunderland, Thomas Allen, mate, of Swanage, Francis Allen, second mate, of Dundee, Richard Grey of Bridlington, Thomas Arthur of Ferryside, Carmarthenshire, Hugh McKenzie of Shetland, Alfred Feer of Hayle, and apprentices Thomas Brooks of Gloucester and Joseph Bray of Hayle. A mast, yards, sails and rigging of a vessel were washed up on Lundy's west coast in the first few days of December 1840. The rough sea prevented anyone recovering it. Perhaps it was from the brig *Alert*.

On the morning of Sunday 11 July 1841 the brig *Eliza*, of St Ives, Clarke master, sank rapidly in a heavy gale near Lundy. The crew of four got aboard their boat but saved nothing apart from what they were wearing. An hour later the brig *Susan*, Fishwick master, hove in sight, bore down, got them aboard and landed them at Appledore.

The *Sarah*, which was bound from Newport to Falmouth, was abandoned in a sinking state between Morte Bay and Lundy on 16 November 1841. Her crew got ashore. Three weeks later the *Odin*, of Hamburg, and *Mary* collided when seeking shelter in Lundy roads. The *Mary*, which was bound from Miramichi (New Brunswick, Canada) to Liverpool, lost seven feet of her stern and was soon waterlogged. Her timber cargo kept her afloat and she was able to reach Penarth roads.

On 19 March 1842 the sloop *Mariner*, of Dartmouth, was bound home from Newport with coal when she foundered in Lundy roads after colliding with the vessel *Ashley*, Captain Frewin, which was bound from Cardiff for Rotterdam. The *Ashley* picked up Captain Thornton and the crew of the *Mariner* and landed them at Ilfracombe where she put in to repair her jib-boom.

The brig *Crescent*, of Exeter, James Payne master, was bound from Swansea to London with 200 tons of coal. On 24 June 1842 she ran into heavy weather when off Padstow and the master, finding she was leaking, decided to run back for Lundy. Before reaching the roads they found seven feet of water in the hold, so abandoned ship and rowed ashore on the morning of the 25th. The brig drove onto the island and broke up. The Trinity House steamer *Argus* landed the crew at Appledore.

The *Rose*, of Cork, was bound from Newport for Rouen when she foundered six miles to the south of Lundy on 31 December 1843. Captain Williams and his crew were picked up and landed at Mumbles on 4 January.

A very heavy storm struck the channel on 3 August 1844 and a few days later two vessels were found bottom up on the west side of Lundy. There was also a good deal of wreckage and a marlin spike marked *Lord Oriel*. The brig *Lord Oriel*, of Falmouth, 123 tons, had sailed from Newport with coal on 1 August bound for Guernsey. Captain James Hugo and his crew of five were drowned. The *St Austell Packet*, of Fowey, had also left Newport and was bound to Charlestown. Captain Henry Nancholes and his two sons were lost. A third vessel which may have sunk to the west of Lundy in that storm was the schooner *Navarino*, of St Ives, master Thomas Paynter, who had his wife aboard.

The *Experiment*, Captain Scantlebury, was bound from Fowey to Newport in ballast. On the evening of 20 August 1845 she was found to be leaking when four miles west of Lundy and sank at 7.30. The crew were picked up by the *Sally*, Tadd master, which was also bound from Fowey for Newport.

On 22 December 1845 the 36 ton smack *Kate*, Newport for Padstow with coal and iron, and the 76 ton schooner *Harmony*, Captain Endicott, Penarth for Bridport with coal, were entering Lundy roads to shelter from the boisterous north-west wind when they collided. The *Kate*'s starboard bow was holed and she filled and sank. Her crew were taken aboard the *Harmony* which had lost her jib-boom and put back to Penarth to repair.

The *Clara*, Captain Atkin, was bound from Cardiff to London and experienced very heavy weather which drove her north. At noon on 28 April 1847 she fell in with the *Mary Isabella*, of Whitehaven, which was bound from Cardiff to Waterford and had lost her sails and was sinking. It took two hours to get Captain McKenzie and his crew on board the *Clara*. The *Mary Isabella* sank at 4.40 about 20 miles north-north-west of Lundy. The *Clara* landed McKenzie and his crew at Milford.

The *Expedition*, of Milford, Raymond master, was bound from Southampton for Gloucester. Leaking badly near Lundy she was abandoned on 18 October 1847 and the crew picked up by a schooner which was "bound foreign". Captain Raymond and his crew were then transferred to a pilot cutter which landed them at Ilfracombe.

The schooner *Ann*, of St Ives, Richards master, was of 150 tons burthen and bound for Cardiff in ballast when driven ashore by a strong wind on the south-west corner of the island at about 11 pm on 2 February 1848. A boy, William Nurse, of Bridgwater, who was a passenger, climbed a mast. The master and crew abandoned in the boat and tried to row round to the landing place on the east side. The boy, who clung to the mast for hours, said that he heard them screaming for help and assumed the boat had capsized. The schooner heeled over and the mast struck the rocks allowing Nurse to climb the cliff and get to the lighthouse. A Pill pilot skiff landed him at Ilfracombe.

Just ten days after the wreck of the *Ann*, the 345 ton barque *Sylphiden*, of Drammen, Norway, ran ashore on the east side of Lundy in dense fog. Captain Guillicksen, the crew and the pilot were assisted up the cliff by lines lowered to them. The vessel, bound from Newport to Havana with steam coal, became a total wreck four days later when the north-east wind rose to near gale force.

The brigantine *Mary Ann*, of Liverpool, sailed from Whitehaven with iron ore for Cardiff on 21 September 1848. She sprang a leak and sank on the afternoon of the 25th about ten miles north-west of Lundy. Captain George Nelson, his sister, and the crew were picked up from their boat by the galliot *Experimenter*, of Bremen, which was bound down channel. The galliot returned up channel and put them aboard the Pill pilot cutter *Albion* which landed them at Cardiff. (A galliot was a type of Dutch or German merchant vessel similar to a ketch used in coastal trade.)

On Tuesday 13 February 1849 the *Catherine*, of St Ives, found the boat of the brig *Valiant*, which was also of St Ives, to the south-east of Lundy and took it to Swansea. The *Maid of Erin*, of Truro, Captain William Harry, put into St Ives having lost her cutwater, bowsprit and jib-boom in a collision between Lundy and Hartland Point on the 12th. It was soon realised that the *Maid of Erin* had collided with the *Valiant* at night drowning her master William Cogar and six crew. The *Valiant* had been bound from Portreath to Swansea with copper ore.

The ship *Archelaus*, J.P. Boutelle master, of and for New York, sailed from Cardiff on 4 November 1849 with a cargo of iron rails. She sprang a leak in going down channel and anchored off Lundy at 2 pm on the 5th. Her crew were taken off by two Bristol pilot cutters. The ship was settling fast on the morning of the 7th and she went down a mile off the island at 8.30. The crew were taken back up channel and landed at Pill by cutter No. 13. The vessels *Britannia* and *Victory* salvaged the masts, rigging and other materials and these were taken ashore by the steamer *Waterwitch*. Then the vessels *Mandamus*, Bell master, *Mary Ann* skippered by Bell's son and *Expedient*, Hall master, worked at the wreck with divers right through the following year and recovered most of the rails which they landed at Ilfracombe. They also raised the ship's anchors. When they had finished the task, the salvage vessels and divers gave a display of their skills one evening in Ilfracombe harbour.

The sloop *Louisa*, of Penzance, Hooper master, was a regular trader to Newport. She sailed from Penzance on 14 February 1850 and sank in Lundy roads on the 18th. Trinity House indicated its position with a green wreck buoy.

The barque *Countess of Bective*, of Sunderland, Captain Davies, bound from Cuba with a cargo of copper ore for Swansea, collided at 10.30 on the evening of 29 May 1850 with the barque *Glenlyon*, of London, bound from Cardiff for San Francisco with coal. The collision occurred about nine miles south-west of Lundy. Eight of the *Countess*'s crew got aboard the *Glenlyon* and the other nine were taken off by a pilot cutter just before the barque sank. The *Glenlyon* was badly damaged – in fact she lost all three masts, her bowsprit, figurehead and cutwater. She was towed by four pilot cutters to Ilfracombe.

Charles Adams, a Bristol pilot, reported that a schooner and a French lugger had been wrecked on Lundy's west coast in the gale of 14 January 1851 drowning all hands: "The rocks were strewn with fragments, but nothing recovered to identify them". The *Shipping and Mercantile Gazette* of 17 February carried an item stating it was feared that the *Louise*, Berget master, bound from Luçon, France, to Gloucester had been lost. It had put into Aber Wrac'h, Brittany, and left there on 10 January and had not since been heard of. It was thought that she must have been the lugger lost at Lundy in January.

The Greek brig *Panaja Eleusa*, Captain Frangoulis Kiliotidis, was bound from Cardiff to Malta with coal when on 22 October 1851 she sprang a leak and was soon sinking twenty miles to the west of Lundy. Her master and crew of nine saved all their belongings, got aboard the two boats and rowed to Tenby, Pembrokeshire. They returned to Cardiff where they would be able to obtain a passage home.

The schooner *Wizard*, of Guernsey, Captain W.F. Guille, was anchored in Lundy roads sheltering from a south-west gale when at 11 pm on 13 January 1852 the wind suddenly shifted to east-north-east. The crew of six attempted to weigh anchor but, with the gale increasing and the vessel driving towards the rocks, they took to the boat and got ashore. The schooner, which had been bound from Bristol to St Michael island in the Azores, sank half an hour later. The next day at low water the vessel was surveyed and condemned. The master sold her where she lay for £40. The day after the *Wizard* was lost the wind dropped and the sea was calm. The brig *Eliza* which was bound from Newport to Hayle with railway iron was leaking badly and sank about six miles to the south-west of Lundy. Captain Tucker and his crew abandoned in the boat and got ashore at Ilfracombe, their home port.

The schooner *Orange Branch*, of Exmouth, was bound from Newport for Plymouth. In the early hours of 23 July 1852 she struck what was believed to be floating wreckage about 14 miles south-west of Lundy and sank very quickly. Captain Balmano and his crew had no chance to save anything. Rowing for more than nine hours they got to Clovelly where they were treated with great kindness by the coastguard and inhabitants.

The schooner *Auspicious*, of and for Hayle from Port Talbot, was well to the west of Lundy on 30 April 1853 when an explosion was heard. Her master saw a vessel about five miles away and sailed to it. When Captain Samuel Rees and his crew arrived they could see that the crew of the brigantine *Ariel*, of Elsfleth (near Bremen), were in the rigging and the vessel was badly damaged. In three trips in their boat the crew of the *Auspicious* rescued eight Germans from the vessel which was now sinking. The *Ariel* had taken in a cargo of coal at Neath or Cardiff (accounts differ) and was bound home. The apprentice had gone into the rope locker with a lighted candle and the cargo exploded. Seaman H. Range, who was standing near the hatchway just aft of the windlass, was hurled overboard and lost. The mate was thrown to the height of the masthead and fell to the deck breaking a leg. The apprentice was badly burnt but survived. The master's dog had also been lost. Captain Warns, master of the *Ariel*, and the seven survivors were landed at St Ives on the evening of 2 May.

The 408 ton barque *Avon*, of Sunderland, Boughtman master, was bound from Santiago, Cuba, for Swansea with copper ore. In dense fog she struck the north-west end of Lundy on the evening of 24 February 1855. The crew abandoned and were picked up by a smack which landed them at Swansea. Sections of the wreck, including the figurehead of a woman with a double row of beads around the neck, floated ashore. A small black dog also swam ashore. The salvage firm of Pulling & Co. were called in and were able to raise a small part of the cargo.

Some ship types mentioned in the text.
Above left: Barque.
Above: Barquentine.
Left: Sloop

1855-1863: Emigrants for New York get no further than Lundy

> **BUTE DOCKS, CARDIFF.**
>
> TO SAIL APRIL 5th, 1855,   FOR NEW YORK.
>
> THE American Clipper Ship "J. R. FOLSOM," 1500 Tons Burthen; ANDREW HEAGAN, Commander. Can accommodate a few Cabin Passengers.
>
> Early application should be made to
> KNAPP & JENKINS, and Co., Bute Docks;
> Or JOSEPH ELLIOTT,
> Emigration Agent, Bute-street.

(*Cardiff and Merthyr Guardian* 17 March 1855)

The ship *Joseph R. Folsom*, 870 tons, Captain Andrew Heagan, was bound from Cardiff for New York with a cargo of railroad iron and emigrants as passengers. She left Penarth roads on the morning of Saturday 14 April 1855 but at midnight struck the Hen and Chickens rocks which lie off the north-west point of Lundy. The vessel's four boats were launched and the twenty-three crew and forty-one emigrants abandoned as the ship began to sink. As the emigrants were in their berths as the ship struck they were mostly in their nightclothes. The four boats were found at dawn at the south-west end of the island by a Bristol pilot cutter, George Buck master. Passengers and crew were all taken aboard and landed on the island where they were taken good care of. Buck then took them all aboard again and landed them back at Cardiff. As his cutter was just thirty feet in length and said to be the smallest of the Bristol boats this was some achievement. At its meeting held in London on the 3rd of May, the Royal National Lifeboat Institution awarded George Buck its thanks and £2, and £1 each to his crew of two men and the boy. There being at least two sides to any story, Captain Heagan claimed that George Buck had done little of note, having charged him £8 to take everyone to Cardiff. One of the emigrants was Samuel Matthews, a Cardiff gardener, who lost the £40 he had taken three years to save to take his wife and six children to America; the Oddfellows opened a fund to assist him.

On Friday 1 June 1855 the *James*, of Llanelli, found the schooner *Hope*, of Chester, derelict twenty miles to the west of Lundy. Three men from the *James* boarded the vessel, pumped her out and sailed her to Llanelli. The *Hope*, which had been bound from Poole to Runcorn with pipeclay, had been struck by heavy seas, drowning the master's wife and one member of the crew. Captain John Piers and two men had been rescued by the barque *Kong Sverre* which landed them at Cardiff.

The SS *Loire*, Captain Cook, left Cardiff for Bordeaux with 750 tons of coal. In dense fog she ran ashore at the north end of Lundy at 3.30 am on Sunday 12 August 1855. By 10 am the ship had broken in two and the stern section slid off the rocks and sank. The crew were picked up by pilot cutters and landed at Cardiff. Richard Huxtable, Lloyd's agent at Ilfracombe, arrived to report on the state of the wreck. The salvage company Forman, of Whitstable, were called in and their divers arrived on the *Wesleyana* on the 15th. They were able to salvage materials from the fore section and if the weather remained moderate hoped to save the ship's engines.

The chasse-marée *Léocadie*, of Nantes, had loaded coal at the Welsh ports for many years. (A chasse-marée was a French fast three-masted lugger traditionally used to deliver fish). At about two o'clock on the morning of 16 November 1855 she was sailing up channel off Lundy on passage from Honfleur for Cardiff, in ballast, when struck by a brig which did not stop. Captain Lemerle and his crew of three worked at the pumps for five hours but could not overcome the leak. They put their belongings, charts and valuables aboard the boat and pulled away as the vessel sank. Rowing to the island they were spotted by the lighthouse keeper and got ashore by farmer Lee. Pilot cutter No. 30 landed them at Ilfracombe where they met Richard Dalley of 4 The Quay who was a French speaker. He directed them to Lt Jones of the preventive service, who was also agent to the Shipwrecked Mariners' Society, and he got them aboard another pilot boat which took them to Cardiff where they able to find a passage home with the aid of the French consul.

The schooner *Choice*, of Bideford, sprang a leak and sank six miles south-south-east of Lundy at 3.15 on the morning of 20 April 1856. There had been no time to launch the long-boat so the crew took to the jolly boat (a smaller vessel). The weather was fine and wind light allowing Captain Williams and his crew to get to Ilfracombe by six o'clock.

The smack *Frederick*, of Dublin, was found abandoned at anchor off Lundy. What became of the crew appears not to have been recorded. She had lost her sails and there were several feet of water over the cargo of coal. She was towed to Clovelly on 4 November 1857 by the *Ranger*, of Bideford, Edward Lee master.

The schooner *Charles*, of Dartmouth, was bound from Plymouth for Llanelli when she was driven ashore at the north-west point of Lundy in the early hours of 13 March 1858. One man jumped onto a rock as the vessel drove past. He was able to hold onto the rock with the woollen comforter he had round his neck. The mate got hold of the jib-boom which parted from the hull and was washed ashore. At dawn he was pleased to see a few sheep above him and climbed the cliff. His feet and hands were cut but he made his way to the lighthouse to raise the alarm. Farm hands took ropes and set off for the scene. They found that the other man had swum ashore and took him to the lighthouse. Captain Marden and four members of the crew had drowned.

The smack *Trident*, of Bristol, bound from Cardiff for Plymouth with coal, was driven ashore on the island by a force nine easterly gale on 9 April 1858. The vessel broke up, drowning the mate, but Captain Davey and the third hand got ashore.

The 143 ton schooner *Plymouth* was bound from Newport to London with a cargo of iron castings. On the afternoon of 29 August 1859 she was twelve miles south by west of Lundy when struck by a heavy gust of wind which caused the cargo to shift and she was soon sinking. Captain Rendle went below to get the boy as the crew launched the boat. As the lad got into the boat one of his fingers was crushed. They had pulled away one hundred yards when the schooner sank. After rowing for two hours they got ashore at Hartland Quay where they were assisted by Captain Stuckley. Surgeon Thomas amputated the lad's finger.

What came to be known as the "Royal Charter Gale" struck Britain on 25 October 1859. This is the report from Lundy sent the next day: "The *Catherine Thomas*, supposed to belong to Nevin, North Wales, has been totally wrecked on this island during the terrific storm that raged in this channel yesterday and last night. No clue has been got to any of the unfortunate crew of the ill-fated vessel: hence it is much to be feared they have met with a watery grave. Another vessel, apparently a brig, is at anchor a few miles off the island, totally dismasted displaying a distress signal, but no means are at hand of rendering any assistance". The next day it was reported that two more wrecks had been discovered. One was a schooner, another a brig or barque, her masts visible at low water. The *Catherine Thomas*, a schooner of 104 tons, had been built at Nefyn, Caernarfonshire in 1850. She was registered at Pwllheli. One of the other wrecks carried a cargo of bar, rail, rod and hoop iron. Four bodies were recovered and buried on the island. Then on 1 November there was another heavy gale. The Bristol pilot cutter *Diligent* No. 39 sank off Lundy. Pilot George Gilmore aged 34, Richard Knight, 58, Grady Marshall, 50, Joseph Simmons, 22, and apprentice John White, 16, drowned. The following day the crew of pilot cutter No. 14 saw the sloop *Peace*, of Brixham, sinking a mile or so to the south-east of the island when bound from Newport for Plymouth with coal. Pilot Edward Craddy and his crew had a real battle with the sea but were able to save Captain Brinham and his crew and land them at Clovelly.

The *Jane*, of Exeter, Seaward master, was bound from Cardiff for Exmouth with railway iron when she was in collision west of Lundy on 8 June 1860 with the *Volusia*, Captain Jarvis, which had also left Cardiff but was bound for Theodosia (Crimea). The *Jane* sank, drowning three of her crew. Two others were picked up by the *Volusia* which put them aboard a Tenby fishing smack the next day.

The 385 ton barque *Sinope*, of Sunderland, was a former Russian vessel seized as a prize during the Crimean War. Leaving Swansea on Wednesday 9 January 1861 with coal for Dieppe, she anchored in Mumbles roads and sailed on Thursday morning. The next day she was eighteen miles west of Lundy when the ends of two planks in the bows became detached and the water was soon gaining on the pumps. At 10 am Captain L.J.H. Stapleton decided to put back up channel. By mid-day the vessel was settling and the boats were launched. Seeing a pilot cutter to windward the ensign was hoisted "union down" and the crew took to the boats. The cutter *True Blue* No. 4 got alongside and pilot Edward Canby boarded by which time there was more than six feet of water in the fore hold. The cutter attempted to tow the barque and the crew returned aboard with all hands to the pumps. By 4 pm there was almost nine feet in the hold and an hour later with eleven feet there, Canby suggested they should abandon ship. Stapleton and his crew boarded the cutter and saw the barque sink at 7.40 four miles to the east of Lundy. They were put ashore at Ilfracombe.

The 101 ton schooner *Lewis Charles*, of Truro, Captain J. Wallis, sailed from Llanelli on 8 February 1861 bound for Penzance. The next day she was in collision during a severe gale off Lundy with the smack *Bottreaux Castle*, Captain Venning, which had left Boscastle bound for Newport. Five of the crew of the schooner got aboard the smack which put in at Padstow badly damaged. The *Lewis Charles* sank, drowning one of her crew.

The brigantine *Valentine*, of Milford, 76 tons, sailed from Waterford on Tuesday 21 May 1861 bound in ballast for Llanelli. Coming up channel on the 23rd there was dense fog. Believing that they were well to the north of Lundy the master William Williams did not use the lead. At two o'clock they realised that they were close to rocks so the boat was launched and they abandoned. The vessel was rolling, struck the rocks and fell over on her starboard side with both masts striking the cliffs.

The crew then saw the lighthouse and rowed round to the east side of Lundy to land. At low water next day they were able to save some of the sails but by Sunday there was no trace of the vessel. The crew were landed at Appledore by the *Ranger*, Captain Dark. It was believed that another vessel had been lost to the west of Lundy at that time as some seamen's chests and wreckage had been washed up.

Bristol pilot cutter No. 13 was ten miles west-south-west of Lundy at about 7 pm on 8 October 1861 when a barque was spotted in distress. Pilot Thomas Carey boarded the *Alert*, of London, 281 tons, which had been built at Java in 1851 and was formerly in the Indian trade. She was now bound from Cardiff to Barcelona with coal and was leaking and sinking in the heavy seas. It took two hours to rescue Captain James, his crew of eleven, and the wife of the second officer. As the last man got aboard the cutter the *Alert* sank. The rescued were landed at Cardiff the next day.

On 13 November 1861 the 93 ton brigantine *Ranger*, of Teignmouth, bound from Neath for Budleigh with culm, was anchored in Lundy roads sheltering from a north-west gale when struck and holed by the brig *Éclair*, of Isigny (Normandy). Captain Charles Shilston and his crew pumped ship for three hours but were forced to abandon shortly before the *Ranger* sank. They were landed at Padstow.

The American brigantine *W.A. Brown* which had left Newport sank twenty miles west of Lundy. Her master and crew of eight took to the boat and were picked up by the steamer *Corinthian* and landed at Cardiff on 28 January 1862.

The schooner *James*, of St Ives, left Swansea with a cargo of coal at 6 pm on 19 March 1862. A few hours after leaving she was found to be leaking and sank late morning the next day to the east of Lundy. Captain Chellew and his crew of four took to the boat with the intention of making Ilfracombe but with the wind blowing strong from the south-east they rowed to Lundy roads. It was now dark so they lay off shore until dawn. As they made for the landing beach the boat capsized in the surf and only seaman William Tanner got ashore. Captain Chellew, William Wallace the mate, John Mathias seaman and the boy William Garvey drowned. Their bodies were recovered and buried in the island churchyard.

The schooner *Wesleyan*, of Goole, Captain Green, left Swansea for Le Havre on 10 June 1862 with a cargo of arsenic and block tin. At 10.30 that evening she was struck by a squall which brought down two masts and swept a man overboard. She was found disabled between Lundy and Hartland the following day. Bristol pilot cutters *Mary Ann* and *Tartar* towed her to Ilfracombe. They were awarded £70 each for salvage.

There was a collision at 2 am on 28 June 1862 about eight miles west-south-west of Lundy between the ship *Screamer*, of Brunswick, U.S.A., and the schooner *Chesapeake*, of Portsmouth. The *Screamer* was in ballast and bound from London for Newport and on the port tack. The *Chesapeake*, bound from Swansea for Cowes with coal, was on the starboard tack. She was struck midships and sank rapidly. Captain Welch, who was below, went down with his vessel. James Styles the mate, seaman Thomas Vounds, and the boy Henry Hoare took hold of ropes which hung from the *Screamer* and were picked up and landed at Newport.

The Cardiff pilot cutter *Ben McCree* foundered off Lundy on 3 November 1862. Her crew landed on the island and were taken to Cardiff three days later by the Pill cutter No. 13.

The 50 ton schooner *Hope*, of Fowey, William Worth master, left Par at 4 pm on 30 December 1863 bound for Swansea with copper ore. The next day the wind was increasing and the flying jib and topgallant sail were taken in. At 4 am they were off the Longships light and reefed the main, top and fore sails. The pumps were checked twice an hour. By 8 am a gale was blowing and there was heavy rain. At 1.30 pm the vessel was labouring and taking a long time to answer the helm. The fore hatch cover was raised and four or five feet of water found in the hold. They were twenty miles west of Lundy. Two ships were seen about four miles off and Worth hoisted the colours into the rigging but the vessels appear not to have seen the signal. The pumps were now choked with ore and by 2.30 the lee rail was under water. Seeing no prospect of saving the *Hope* the boat was hoisted out and four crew and two passengers abandoned at three o'clock and rowed to a schooner which picked them up. It was the *Why Not*, Captain Jenkins, bound from Llanelli for Plymouth. The *Hope* was seen to sink and the *Why Not* landed the survivors at Penzance on 2 January. The agent of the Shipwrecked Mariners' Society arranged their journey home.

The Shipwrecked Mariners' Society

THE SHIPWRECKED FISHERMEN AND MARINERS' Royal Benevolent Society, or Shipwrecked Mariners' Society as it's more commonly known, was founded in 1839 to assist the survivors of shipwreck and to support the widows and orphans of those lost at sea. Today the Society is one of the largest maritime charities operating throughout the UK and Ireland, and its main function is benevolence and the payment of discretionary grants through its countrywide network of Honorary Agents.

The Society's flag, a St George's cross with the letters SFMS in the quadrants and, originally, a number, was displayed by ships and their position reported by the coastguard to the *Shipping and Mercantile Gazette* in London. Some vessels also bore the Society's flag and number painted on a board to provide a more permanent means of identification. This proved its worth when, in 1851, the *William*, of Kirkaldy, foundered off Ballywater, County Down. The board was the only item of the vessel recovered, to prove her identity, and enabled the Society to assist dependants of the lost crew.

Individual mariners, as well as ships, could be members of the Society. A medallion was issued with a space for a membership number to be scratched on and many seafarers wore the medallion around their necks. An example of the medallion is shown on p.42. The membership scheme ended in 1978.

The Society has around sixty collecting boxes to raise funds for its charitable work in the form of old sea-mines *(left)*. They were originally donated by the Admiralty for use as collection boxes in recognition of the Society's significant help to thousands of shipwrecked survivors during World War II. They are sited in coastal towns all around the UK, including one or two on outer islands.

1863-1865: No blockade running for *Iona* or *Matilda*

THE 365 ton paddle steamer *Iona* was built at Govan in 1863 for service on the Clyde. The Board of Trade certificate allowed her to take 1,352 passengers to Dunoon but just 723 to Ardrishaig. Soon after building she was sold for £18,000 to someone who represented the Confederate States in the American Civil War. Her builders, J. & G. Thomson, strengthened her at a cost of £4,000 and plated over her side ports. She left Glasgow on 16 January 1864 with Thomas Hoare Chapman as master and Joseph Gray as first mate, there being 39 hands all told. She was said to be bound for Nassau in the Bahamas with the intention of working as a blockade runner. (This vessel is often referred to as *Iona II* to distinguish her from a predecessor and a later vessel of the same name. When built and launched, she was simply *Iona*.)

The *Iona* put into Waterford at 9 pm on the 18th to discharge the pilot and left there on Sunday 24 January. She next put into Queenstown (Cobh) and intended leaving there at noon on the 28th but the firemen refused duty saying that they did not think the vessel seaworthy. The police were informed and came aboard taking thirteen men ashore. Four returned aboard and the other nine appeared in court and were sentenced to ten weeks in prison. The second engineer commented that it was quite common for firemen to "hook it" from ships after they had received a month's advance of their pay. The master signed on another nine firemen and the ship sailed at 12.30 pm on the 30th with the intention of calling at Madeira before making the Atlantic crossing. When at Queenstown a loose rivet had been found under the centre of the stoke-hold but this was put right before sailing.

By noon on Sunday 31 January the wind was blowing hard from the south-west, a heavy sea was running and the steamer labouring. At 2 pm the course was changed for Milford Haven. By midnight there was a heavy gale. The vessel was rolling and a good deal of water was getting aboard. By the next morning she was flooded to a depth of two feet. All hands were now pumping or passing coal from the main hold to the bunkers. The bilge pumps became choked with coal dust. The vessel was then to the south-west of Lundy. By 6 pm there were six feet of water in the holds and an hour later the forward fires were put out by the rising water. The after fires were kept going by tearing down the wooden bulk heads and burning them with grease. The engines were stopped at 11.30 when the ship was a short distance to the east of Lundy. Both anchors were let go, blue lights shown and rockets fired. The crew left in the boats and got aboard Alfred Ray's Pill pilot cutter No. 32. Later, eight men got back aboard the *Iona* with Chapman and Gray but found that the water was just three feet below deck level and over the cabin table. They remained aboard until a few minutes before the vessel sank. The crew were landed at Ilfracombe by the pilot cutter. The wreck of the *Iona* lies east of Gull Rock off Lundy's east coast. See also p.65.

George Barbour, a shipwright surveyor to the Board of Trade, had inspected the *Iona* when she was being built and saw her when being adapted. He concluded that she was not seaworthy and he would have withheld the certificate if applied for. His grounds were that Lloyd's Register rules were that the minimum length of a vessel was to be nine times the depth and the maximum length was to be fourteen times the depth. The length of the *Iona* was a little over twenty-seven times her depth and this gave weakness. Her frame was too light and the hull was not sufficiently rigid to withstand the shocks of the sea and when pitching and rolling, her plate ends and rivets would have a tendency to move and leak. She was deficient in longitudinal strength so if supported midships on the crest of a wave or the ends on two waves she would bend or strain.

The Board of Trade inquiry absolved the master from blame in relation to the loss of the *Iona*. The jailed firemen were released from prison having served four weeks.

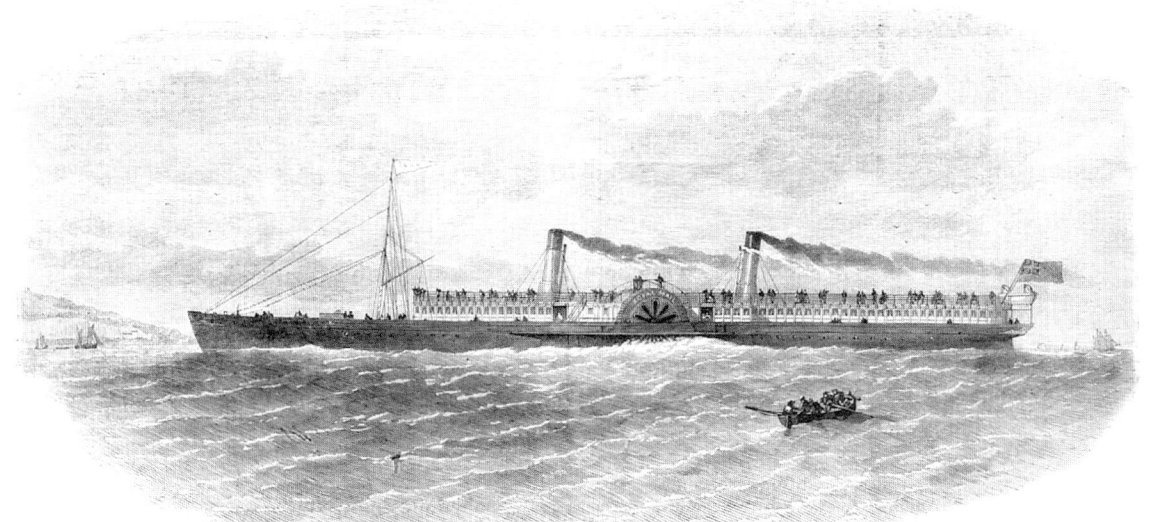

The paddle-steamer *Iona* wrecked at Lundy (*Illustrated London News* 12 September 1863)

The 156 ton brigantine *Shannon*, of and from Newport, with railway iron for Bari (Italy) was three days out and west of Lundy when at 10.45 on the morning of 5 February 1864 her foretopsail parted in the high wind. A heavy sea struck the starboard bow at 11.30 and when the pumps were sounded there were three feet of water in the hold. All hands worked at the pumps and the course was changed for Bideford. The water gained on the pumps and by 2.40 pm the vessel was dull in the water and seas breaking over the deck. Ten miles west by north of Lundy the crew took to the boat and as they pulled away the *Shannon* sank. They made little progress in rowing for Lundy but at 6 pm were picked up by the barque *Tertius* bound from Cardiff for Malta. The next day they transferred to the Norwegian barque *Eidswold* which landed them at Youghal on the Irish coast on 8 February. Captain Trew and his crew got back to Newport by steamer on the 11th.

Another vessel which was intended as a blockade runner for the Confederates was the 544 ton SS *Matilda*. She left Glasgow on 26 March 1864 and arrived at Cardiff on the 28th to take on a cargo of coal and steel. She left Cardiff for Bermuda on the afternoon of 4 April with a crew of about thirty and a Major Pearson of the Confederate artillery. The master was W.G. Pinchon and the pilot John Wright. By 8.30 the ship was a few miles south-west of the Scarweather lightship, her course west by north ½ north, the weather was clear, her speed ten knots. The weather became hazy and by 10 pm it was very thick so the speed was reduced to six knots. By 10.40 the fog was dense so Wright ordered dead slow. He was hoping to hear the Lundy fog gun but didn't. There were two men forward as lookouts and one shouted "Something ahead!" at which the pilot ordered "Stop her". Before the order could be carried out the ship struck Seal Rock off the northern end of Lundy's east coast. The carpenter reported two feet of water in the fore hold. All hands boarded the pilot cutter which was towed astern. A short time later the master returned to save his instruments and found eight feet of water in the engine room. The crew were taken aboard the tug *J.P. Bidder* and landed at Cardiff. Efforts were then made to raise the *Matilda* but by the end of April it was realised it was a lost cause, heavy seas having washed away a considerable portion. Hugh Palmer, of Caernarfon, was then called in and by the end of September he and his divers had recovered the engines which were returned to the builders in Glasgow. The Board of Trade inquiry returned Captain Pinchon's certificate but said that he should have told the pilot that the ship's three compasses did not agree and varied by as much as two points!

Sale of the wrecked *Matilda* (*Glasgow Herald* 3 May 1864)

> **TO ENGINEERS, STEAMSHIP BUILDERS, DIVERS, AND OTHERS.**
>
> IMPORTANT UNRESERVED SALE, BY PUBLIC AUCTION, OF A MARINE STEAM ENGINE,
>
> 150 Nominal Horse-Power, by Henderson, Coulbourn & Co., of Renfrew, built this year, fitted with Oscillating Cylinder, Cog Driving Wheel, and the most recently improved Double or Twin Screws, with Round Tubular Boilers, of the best construction, complete;
>
> Together with the HULL and CARGO of the Iron-Built S.S. "MATILDA," of Glasgow, launched last month, 544 gross, 389 net reg. tonnage; length, 210 feet; beam, 25 feet; depth, 12 feet.
>
> MESSRS. JAMES MARYCHURCH & CO. have instructions to Sell, by Auction, for the benefit of whom it may concern, on Friday the 6th day of May, 1864, the ENGINES, HULL, CARGO, SPARS, and MATERIALS, of the S.S. "MATILDA," of Glasgow, where she now lies on the Rocks at Lundy Island, in the Bristol Channel. The Wreck being fixed where there is only a depth of 12 feet at low water spring tides, is well situated for carrying on the necessary operations for removing the Machinery, discharging the Cargo, and ultimately raising the Hull.
>
> The MATILDA was constructed with a special view to attain a high rate of speed, and to secure which the most recent improvements have been adopted in the construction of the Engines, regardless of expense.
>
> A Steamer will leave the Pier Head, Cardiff, at Eight o'clock precisely on Friday Morning, arriving at the Wreck about One o'clock, affording an opportunity to all who may think fit to inspect for themselves the position of the Vessel.
>
> The Sale will take place as soon as practicable after arrival at the Wreck. The Materials, consisting of Copper Piping and Sundry Engine Stores, will be Sold at Cardiff, on Saturday the 7th of May, at Eleven o'clock in the Forenoon.
>
> Further particulars may be obtained of Mr. Christopher Rapier, Shipbroker, Bute Crescent, Cardiff; or of the Auctioneers, 15 Bute Crescent.

> **To Bristol Channel Pilots and Others.**
>
> THE SCHOONER "SUPERIOR," of Whitehaven, was run into on Saturday Night, 1st October, about 9 p.m., near Lundy, by a Screw Steamer. Any one giving information which may lead to the name of the Steamer, will be rewarded on application to THOMAS RUSSELL, Ship Broker, Cardiff.
>
> Cardiff, 6th October, 1864.   5805

(*Cardiff Times* 7 October 1864)

The schooner *Superior*, of Whitehaven, was bound from Sligo to Cardiff with a cargo of meal. At about 9 pm on Saturday 1 October 1864 she was off Lundy when struck by a steamer. Totally disabled, she drifted back down channel in the easterly wind and eventually went ashore at Killoughter, County Wicklow. John Ennis a young seaman was drowned. Hoping to discover the identity of the steamer, Thomas Russell, a Cardiff shipbroker, placed adverts in the *Shipping and Mercantile Gazette* and *Cardiff Times*.

A gale from the south-west struck on 16 November 1864 and by the following day had risen to storm force ten and veered to the north-west. The Bristol pilot cutter *Helen* No. 28 put pilot Charles Porter aboard the ship *Far West*, of Newport, which had lost her anchors and had her foremast sprung by the storm. The ship was bound from Callao (Peru) to Waterford with guano but had been driven into the Bristol Channel. It eventually got safely to port. Then pilot William Comerford brought a ship down channel and boarded the *Helen* to the west of Lundy. Other Bristol cutters were sheltering in Lundy roads and their crews kept a look out for the *Helen* but she did not appear. A few days later parts of the cutter were found. Those who died were pilots John Thomas and William Comerford, apprentices James Shepherd and Stephen Turner and John Smith, aged fourteen, the son of a pilot. They were all from Pill and services were held in the village in memory of them.

Captain Davey of the *Mary Maria*, of Teignmouth, arrived at Liverpool and reported that at 7 am on 29 April 1865 they fell in, about eight miles west-north-west of Lundy, with the schooner *Sandwich Bay*, of Dartmouth, with her ensign flying union down. The vessel had been abandoned. They stood by for a few hours, hoping to board her, but with the wind and sea increasing and the schooner settling they abandoned the idea and headed for Liverpool. The schooner, of which John Salisbury was master, had left Llanelli with a cargo of steam coal for Margate on the 28th. The crew were obliged to batten down the hatches in heavy seas. The next day, when they were six miles north-west of Lundy, the deck blew up and the pumps became choked. The crew took to the boat and were picked up by the *T.G.V.*, of Jersey, which landed them at Llanelli.

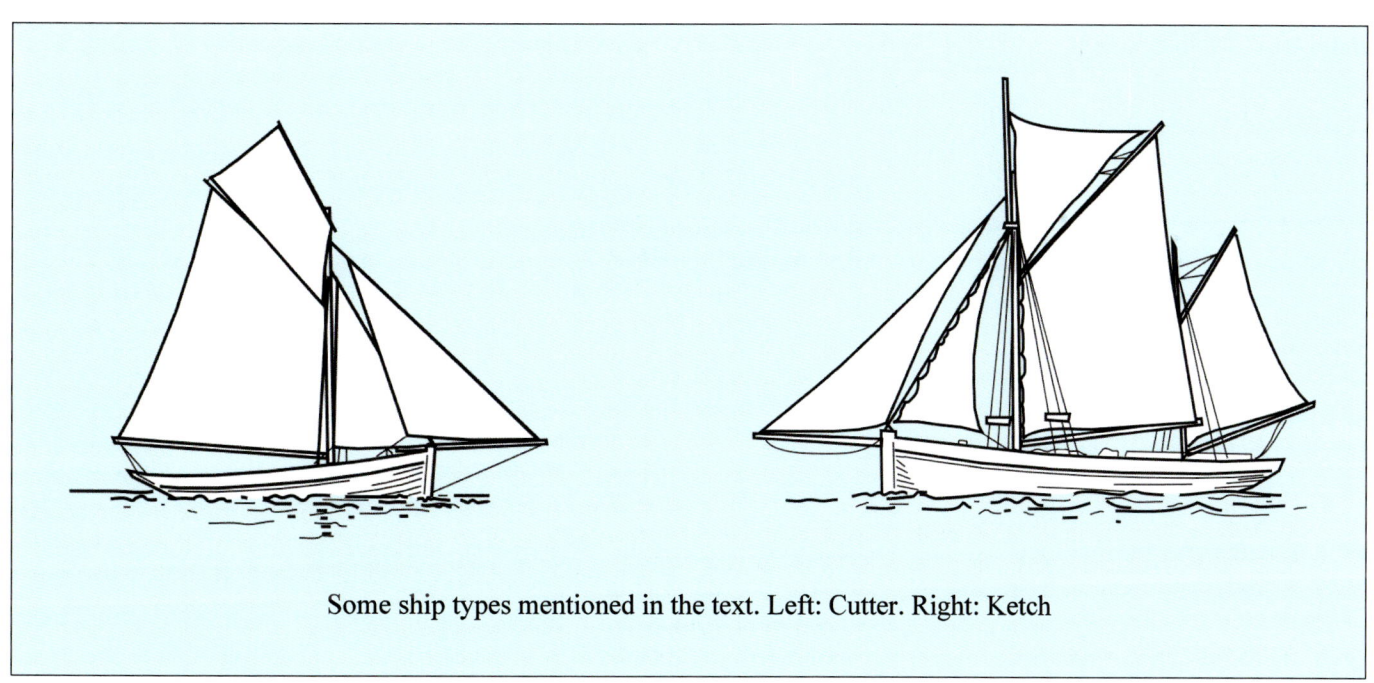

Some ship types mentioned in the text. Left: Cutter. Right: Ketch

1865-1876: Nineteen drown on the *Hannah More*

THE 1,129 ton ship *Hannah More*, of Liverpool, James Houghton master, had taken emigrants to Australia in 1865. She then sailed to the Chincha islands off Peru and loaded guano. She was bound for Queenstown (Cobh) for orders as to where to discharge the cargo. The *Shipping and Mercantile Gazette* of Friday 12 January 1866 carried the item: "Ilfracombe Jan 11 NE strong gale. The *Hannah More*, Houghton, from the Chinchas for Queenstown, has brought up in Lundy roads and anchored with some sails blown away. A channel pilot from her has been informed that she is bound for London, but the gale is so strong at north-east that he cannot proceed to the island with the information."

William Thomas, the ship's sailmaker, wrote a report of the wreck: "We left Callao 22 September. Met very heavy weather which forced us past Queenstown, where we were to call for orders, and sheltered under the lee of Lundy on 8 January. Remained there until the 10th. At 6 pm the weather thick, wind north-east strong. We tried to raise the anchor but failed. Got out the port anchor and veered 120 fathoms on each. At 5 am on Thursday the port cable parted and starboard cable went twenty minutes later. We all tried to get her clear of the island but failed and she drove on Rat Island and was a total wreck in half an hour. I and four hands were taken off by a boat from the island manned by Thomas Sanders and Samuel Jarman who did so at great risk. Seaman E.A. Noliscott swam ashore and was pulled out by Albert Escourt". The men who survived were William Shore, John Hiley, John Williams, John Scott, E.A. Noliscott and William Thomas. Those who drowned were the master, the three mates, and fifteen seamen. Bad weather kept the survivors on Lundy until Saturday 20 January when they were landed at Clovelly.

On the morning of 16 January 1866 Cardiff pilots Grimes and Rosser were off Lundy, seeking inbound ships, when they saw distress signals. They found the badly damaged barque *Anne Williams*, bound for Liverpool with timber from Manzanillo, Cuba. The pilot yawl collided with the ship and sank. Grimes and Rosser were taken aboard the *Anne Williams* which docked at Bristol.

The 1,295 ton screw-steamer *Hector*, of Sunderland, Captain Newton, Liverpool to Newport in ballast, struck Lundy in thick fog on 28 March 1866. Her jib-boom, bowsprit, and figurehead were carried away and the stem twisted. She steamed up to Cardiff where she was put on the grid-iron and repaired.

Pill pilot cutter No. 3 was twenty miles west of Lundy on the afternoon of 27 November 1866 when her crew caught sight of a vessel flying a flag on the mizzen mast and looking very low in the water. Getting alongside, pilot William Rowlands advised Captain Thomas Abbott to abandon ship. Abbott and the crew of the barque *Brothers*, of Guernsey, 379 tons, got aboard the boats. The barque, which was bound from Swansea to Dieppe with 630 tons of coal, sank an hour later. The cutter took the boats in tow and landed the crew at Padstow the next day. The Board of Trade inquiry was held at Weymouth and found that Captain Abbott, who had over forty years' experience, was in default for not having made for the nearest port as soon as he realised that the pumps were not coping with the leak. His certificate was suspended for three months. (Suspension of a certificate meant that the seafarer could not work and therefore lost his earnings for that time.)

The 97 ton schooner *Bicton*, of and for St Ives, sailed from Neath with 163 tons of coal on 2 April 1867. When seven miles east-north-east of Lundy she was on the starboard tack and labouring in the cross sea; Captain Christopher Woolcock found she had sprung a leak. By 2 am on the 3rd the water was over the cabin sheets and the boat was launched and towed astern. With the vessel settling the crew abandoned and she went down stern first half an hour later. At 3.30 they fell in with the Cardiff pilot cutter *Stranger* No. 32, Richards master, which took them aboard and landed them at Ilfracombe at 11 o'clock. Ending his report, which was published in *the Shipping and Mercantile Gazette*, Captain Woolcock desired to return his thanks for the great kindness he and his crew received on board the *Stranger*.

Many vessels were sheltering from a gale in Lundy roads on 21 April 1867. The brig *Oscar,* which was bound from Newport to Southampton, parted her cables and drove into the London barque *Queen of Peace*, which was bound from Cardiff to Martinique. The brig sank as her crew abandoned and were picked up by the pilot skiff *Vixen* and put aboard the barque which returned up channel and docked at Bristol for repair having lost her bowsprit.

In the Lundy Field Society annual report of 1967 Michael Bouquet mentions the barque *Alphonse*, abandoned after collision. In fact this was the barque *Adolphe*, 198 tons, of and from St Malo (Brittany) for Cardiff, which was in collision with a Swedish vessel in the early hours of 7 October 1867 to the east of Lundy. Captain Louis Alexander Hardy and five members of the crew got aboard the Swedish vessel believing that the barque was sinking; four others abandoned in the jolly boat and landed on the Devon coast. The badly damaged *Adolphe* was boarded by a crew from Ilfracombe and sailed up to Cardiff.

The 643 ton barque *Columba*, of Spezia near Genoa, Captain Jouphe Borrone, sailed from Cardiff on the morning of 26 October 1867 bound for Point de Galle, Ceylon, with a cargo of steam coal. The pilot left near Lundy and the vessel made good progress to the west but at midnight the strong wind and heavy seas made the master run back up channel. At about four o'clock a very heavy sea broke over the barque smashing in a hatchway. Then it was realised the vessel had begun to leak. Two Bristol pilots, Edward Canby and John Adams, saw the vessel one mile off the north end of Lundy flying a distress signal. The master ran the barque ashore before the pilot boats reached her. Canby and Adams boarded the vessel to offer assistance but the master declined so they left and returned to their cutters. The pilots noticed that the vessel was on fire that evening and had burnt to the water line when they left. The hull and all her materials and stores were put up for auction in Cardiff just over a week later.

Sale of the *Columba*
(*Cardiff Times* 9 November 1867)

PORT OF CARDIFF.

MR. G. SULLY has received instructions to SELL by AUCTION, for the benefit of whom it may concern, at his Sale Room, west end of James street, Bute Docks, on THURSDAY, NOVEMBER 14th, 1867, at Eleven o'clock in the Forenoon, the HULL of the Italian BARQUE "Columba," of Genoa, according to such conditions as shall then and there be produced, now wrecked on the Beach, Lundy Island, where she ebbs up, and can be inspected; 643 tons register, 973 tons burthen, coppered and copper fastened. The ship was quite new, and on her first voyage, when wrecked.

On FRIDAY, Nov. 15th, at same time and place, the whole of the GROUND TACKLE, SPARS, WIRE RIGGING, ROPES, SAILS, STORES, &c., &c., will be Sold, and all without reserve.

The Auctioneer particularly calls attention to the above Sale, and solicits punctual attendance.

Further information may be obtained from Messrs. Morteo and Penco, shipbrokers; or Mr. Geo. Sully, Mount Stuart square, Cardiff,   2725

The schooner *West Dock*, of Waterford, was wrecked on Lundy's west coast on 22 December 1867. The incident barely got a mention in the press but James Power, one of the seamen, took an action against Captain Curran to pay him his wages. Power had been taken on at the monthly rate of £2-15s and sought the £1-13s-10d due him for the nine days that he was aboard and the four days they were on the island before being taken off. He did get the £1-13-10 plus his costs.

The SS *East Anglian*, of Liverpool, 268 tons, Captain Edward Dempsey, left Porthcawl on Sunday 12 January 1868 with 448 tons of coal for Plymouth. That evening the wind rose to gale force. Dempsey reported that heavy seas were running all night and at 1 pm on the 13th he put the ship on the starboard tack, labouring heavily and shipping great quantities of water. The pumps were carefully operated. At 8 pm the seas went down a little and Lundy light was seen about twenty miles to the east-north-east. Dempsey got the ship before the wind and set the square sail and ran for Lundy roads but the water was gaining on the engine room and stokehold. The men then used buckets to bail out the stokehold. Soon after midnight the gale blew stronger from the west-south-west and the water put the fires out and the engine was stopped. The ship broached to. Lundy light was now eight miles to the north-east, the sea making fearful breaches over the ship. Seeing no chance of saving the vessel, the crew launched the two boats and left at about 1 am on the 14th. They reached Lundy at 7.30 am and were assisted ashore. Captain Dempsey went to the store to buy food but was "refused with most abusive language". He and his sixteen crew were well looked after by Miss Heaven who provided them with refreshments and by William Heaven, "lord of the manor", who found clothes for them. They then got aboard the Bristol pilot cutter No. 32, Ray master, and were landed at Swansea at eleven on Wednesday evening.

The smack *Caroline*, William King master, loaded a cargo of granite at Lundy quarry on 18 February 1868 and then anchored in the roads. She began to leak that evening and next morning she was run ashore. Her crew got ashore with the assistance of the islanders. The granite was to have been taken to Fremington.

The schooner *J.C.A.*, of Padstow, Captain James Strout, was bound from Neath to Plymouth with coal when she collided with the schooner *Trelissick*, of St Ives, eight miles south-west of Lundy at 3.30 on the morning of 24 April 1868. The *Trelissick*, which was bound from Portreath to Pembrey, Carmarthenshire, with copper ore, sank an hour later. Her crew, two of whom were injured, were picked up by the *J.C.A.* and landed at Padstow where they were taken care of by the Shipwrecked Mariners' Society.

Morgan, the master of a Cardiff pilot cutter, saw a smack flying a distress signal to the west of Lundy on 21 August 1868. The cutter bore down and Morgan was told the smack, *Gwydir Castle*, had a leak in the stern. The cutter towed her towards the island as her crew worked at the pumps. After three hours the leak became so bad that the crew had to abandon. They were landed at Cardiff.

Soon after five on the morning of Sunday 23 August 1868 a barque was seen a few miles south-east of Lundy. It appeared to be trying to seek shelter in the lee of the island from the heavy south-west gale that was blowing. The vessel rolled heavily and then foundered. Seeing this, the crew of the pilot skiff *Lady Clive,* which was in the roads, slipped the anchors and made for the spot under a heavy press of canvas. They sailed through the race of broken sea which ran past the south of the island and entered a good deal of wreckage where they found one man. He had been clinging to a spar for about forty minutes and was the sole survivor of the *Admiral*, of Jersey, which had left Swansea with coal for Dieppe on Thursday. Heavy seas had carried away the vessel's bowsprit and holed the deck. Her crew had worked at the pumps for forty-eight hours before the vessel sank drowning the master and six hands. George Maule had witnessed the rescue and reported it to the Royal National Lifeboat Institution. Richard Lewis, secretary of the institution, sent Maule a draft for £6 asking him to give William Selway, the *Lady Clive*'s master, £3, the mate £2 and the boy £1 as a token of regard for their gallant effort.

On Tuesday 1 September 1868 the brigantine *Nautilus*, of West Hartlepool, was sailing down channel with a cargo of coal from Llanelli bound for London. She was four miles from Lundy at dusk when hit by the barque *Sparfield*, of Nantes, which was bound from St Nazaire for Penarth. The barque's bows struck the *Nautilus* abaft the main rigging and cut her in two. The master, William Pratt, and the mate seized the barque's rigging and got aboard as their vessel went down. The four hands who were below deck were drowned. The barque lost her jib-boom and fore-topmast but was able to dock at Penarth.

The schooner *Swift*, of Teignmouth, 81 tons, Captain George Carlisle, left Cardiff with coal for Plymouth on 3 October 1868. By the 5th they were ten miles north-north-east of the Longships when it came on to blow hard from the south-west. The vessel was labouring and taking in a good deal of water. The master decided to run back up channel to shelter at Mumbles. They hove-to for eight hours fifteen miles west of Lundy but with the gale getting stronger Carlisle thought it unlikely the schooner would reach Mumbles so anchored in Lundy roads on the 7th. The crew were exhausted by working full time at the pumps and abandoned as the *Swift* foundered at 2 am on Thursday 8 October. They pulled ashore on the island half an hour later.

George Steel was master of the 78 ton schooner *Julia*, of and for Penzance, which left Swansea with coal on 27 October 1868. The vessel was twenty miles west of Lundy when the west-south-west wind reached gale force. The crew reefed the sails and bore up for Lundy and anchored in the roads. The *Julia* was then leaking badly so they were pumping continuously. On the afternoon of the 31st the schooner began to roll heavily. Captain Steel had gone ashore on Lundy to find provisions and when he returned the mate reported the vessel was sinking. The crew abandoned at midnight and in five minutes the *Julia* sank. They were taken aboard the smack *Diamond*, of Jersey, which was also anchored in the roads. Captain Steel and his crew were landed at Ilfracombe by a pilot boat on the evening of 2 November.

The brig *Apphia*, of Dartmouth, 183 tons, was bound from Cardiff for Dakar, West Africa. Captain William Prowse reported: "We left Cardiff on 27 January 1869. At 8 pm 30th the weather overcast the wind south-south-west fresh to moderate gale. At anchor in Lundy roads with 45 fathoms chain on port bow. A brig, the *Hermina* of Maassluis, Holland, was anchored half a mile south-east of me. That evening she parted her chain and in five minutes struck me on the port bow. His starboard anchor being on the rail hooked my fore rigging. The Dutchman was alongside half an hour breaking in my stanchions, main rail and bulwarks. Then she dropped astern and foundered and drew my vessel down on its port side to the water's edge. Smashed my boat with three hands in it to pieces. We hauled the men on deck with ropes. It took an hour to disconnect their anchor from us. Had the brig sunk in deeper water she would have pulled us down too. Two men and a boy had got from the Dutchman to us and survived but the six on the *Hermina* were drowned. I brought my vessel back to Penarth considerably damaged on 2 February".

The schooner *Richard*, of and for Teignmouth, with 133 tons of culm from Briton Ferry entered Lundy roads at 4.30 am on 14 February 1869. She struck a hidden wreck, probably the *Hermina*, and was soon sinking. Captain James Adams and his crew got aboard the SS *Express*, of Hayle, which landed them at Cardiff on the 15th.

The 38 ton Bristol pilot cutter *Albion* No. 9 left Pill on 13 March 1869. She put into Ilfracombe and left there on the 16th. After cruising the channel seeking incoming vessels she anchored in Lundy roads on the morning of the 19th. John Paine, her master, reported that "between three and four that afternoon the wind which had been squally from south-west suddenly veered in a heavy squall to north-north-east and blew a full gale. She began to drag so I veered out the cable to 70 fathoms but the anchor still coming home and vessel nearing the shore I was obliged to slip. Foresail hoisted but split and only chance was to run before the wind and take the shore. When the *Albion* struck two fishermen assisted us ashore by hauling us through the breakers with a line". The *Albion* became a total loss.

The brig *Belinda*, 156 tons, of Weymouth, Joseph Randall master, was bound from London to Swansea with 220 tons of copper ore. Struggling against the west wind she put into Falmouth for a few days and left there on 5 April 1869. At 8 pm on the 6th the weather was thick and the wind moderate from the south-west. The brig was running up channel, under double-reefed topsails, when the crew heard the Lundy fog gun just the once and saw they were very close. Randall ordered the helm hard down and attempted to stay the brig, but she missed stays and, there being no room to wear ship, she struck broadside on close to the south-west end of the island. With the vessel breaking up they abandoned and rowed to the smack *Argo*, of Minehead, which was lying in the roads. The next day they landed on the island. Told they would have to find their own provisions they returned to the *Argo* whose master Captain Pulsford, though bound for Plymouth, landed them at Ilfracombe where they stayed at the "White Hart" before leaving for home. The salvage cutter *Providence* succeeded in raising some of the ore from the *Belinda* which was sunk in four fathoms at low water.

The brig *Margaret*, of St John's, had been built at New Perlican, Newfoundland, in 1853. She left the West Bute Dock, Cardiff, with coal for Montevideo on 3 April 1869 and anchored in Penarth roads overnight. She sailed next morning but collided with the German brig *Orion* which was also anchored in the roads. A tug towed the *Margaret* into Penarth dock where she underwent repairs, having lost her mainmast in the collision. She sailed from Penarth on 18 April to resume her voyage. The next day, when twenty miles to the west of Lundy, the wind rapidly increased from the west. At 11 am a heavy sea struck when she was on the port tack. The well was sounded and found to be making water. (The well was the lowest part of the hull interior where any water would collect.) On the 20th the wind moderated but the leak was increasing. The ship was now labouring heavily and leaking about ten inches per hour. On the 21st Captain William Kendell decided to run back up channel as the leak was steadily getting worse and the crew constantly at the pumps. Then on the 22nd the crew went aft and told Kendell that they were refusing to work at the pumps and wished to take to the boats. The well was sounded and indicated nearly five feet of water in the hold. The boats were launched and all hands got aboard and lay astern. The Newport pilot cutter *Speedwell* No. 19 came alongside. The brig was drifting up channel and Kendell got back aboard a few times and found she was slowly sinking. At 12.45 pm the *Margaret* settled by the stern and sank about 12 miles west-north-west of Lundy. Her crew were taken on board the *Speedwell* which landed them at Ilfracombe.

James Morgan, boatswain of the schooner *Storm Nymph*, of Hayle, wrote a report of the vessel's passage from Porthcawl to Portreath. They left Porthcawl on 20 September 1869 with 200 tons of coal. At 4.30 am next day, when they were south-east of Lundy, they saw a brig running down towards them with a signal of distress flying. The schooner hove to and when the brig was in hailing distance its master asked them to stand by him as his vessel was sinking. Captain Reid of the *Storm Nymph* advised him to make sail and head for the lee of Lundy. At 9 am, with both vessels under way, Morgan and the schooner's mate took the boat and boarded the brig which was the *Ver*, of Sunderland, Captain Anderson, bound from Swansea for Trouville (Normandy). They assisted the brig's crew at the pumps but the water, which was near six feet deep, gained on them. They then moved the master's wife and two children to the schooner. With one more hand they again boarded the *Ver* but there was now eight feet of water in her. With no chance of saving the brig, Captain Anderson and his crew abandoned in the boat and moved to the *Storm Nymph* with all their belongings. As the schooner left they saw the brig go down. The *Storm Nymph* reached Portreath at 8 pm on the 22nd to land the rescued and unload her cargo.

Some writers have the smack *Eliza*, of Plymouth, listed as being wrecked near Lundy on 30 December 1869 but where she sank is not known. The story began in Swansea Bay on the morning of Saturday 1 January 1870. Oyster dredgermen David Rees and William Thomas noticed a boat drifting near their skiff. They drew alongside and found a young man lying dead in the bottom. The body was taken ashore and handed over to the police. The boat had "*Eliza*, Plymouth" on the transom. The schooner *Lubentia*, also of Plymouth, was in Swansea's South Dock and crew member Edward Cottle went to the mortuary and identified the body as that of William John Brown, aged about 18, the mate of the *Eliza*. The smack had left Bideford, with a cargo of gravel for the buildings being erected on Flat and Steep Holm. The *Eliza* had been crewed by Captain Brown and his three sons.

The schooner *Bessie Mitchell*, of Swansea, 98 tons, sailed from Briton Ferry on 8 February 1870 with 165 tons of tin plate valued at £3,500 bound for Southampton. At about 5 am on the 9th the vessel was 10 miles west-south-west of Lundy when a green light was seen ahead and ten minutes later a barque was seen running up channel. Having ported his helm the schooner's master, John Thomas, hailed the barque and asked her crew to port their helm. The barque struck the schooner on its port quarter carrying away its rails, bulwarks and stanchions and smashing the wheel. The wreckage was cleared and a tackle attached to the tiller. The barque did not stop. It was decided to put back for Briton Ferry. By 7 am they were abreast Lundy and the schooner leaking so badly they steered for Caldy Island intending to run her ashore. By nine o'clock the water was over the cabin floor and soon after ten the crew abandoned. The *Bessie Mitchell* sank fifteen miles south of Caldy. The crew landed at Manorbier near Tenby at 1.30 pm and got home by train with the assistance of the Shipwrecked Mariners' Society. The barque was identified as the *Volage*, 731 tons, New York to Sharpness with timber. The case was heard at the Admiralty court and found in favour of the owner of the *Bessie Mitchell*.

> **WRECK OF THE BESSIE MITCHELL.**
>
> TENDERS for SALVAGE are invited from Divers and Others, to RAISE the CARGO of TIN-PLATES (165 tons) of the Bessie Mitchell, sunk in the Bristol Channel, midway between Caldy Island and Lundy Island.
> Apply to PHELPS, JAMES, and CO., Liverpool.   5974

(*Western Mail* 1 June 1870)

The barque *Asterias*, of Boston U.S.A., had loaded 1,230 tons of steam coal at Cardiff and was bound for Hong Kong. At 9.45 on the morning of Saturday 21 May 1870 she was west of Lundy when there was a huge explosion. It was said that two men had gone into the after hold to look for something with a naked flame. John Johnson, who was at the wheel, was flung into the air, fell into the sea, and not seen again. The master, James W. Sloan, was found collapsed between the main and mizzen masts and died in twenty minutes. Another man was flung into the sea but took hold of a line and was hauled aboard. The barque was now on fire so the first mate, George Deacon of Cardiff, ordered the boats away. The twelve survivors, three of whom had suffered burns, left taking Captain Sloan's body with them. The tug *Dandy*, of Falmouth, saw the vessel on fire five miles south-west of Milford Haven that evening. Two hours after abandoning, the *Asterias*' survivors were found fifteen miles west of Lundy by the brigantine *Success*, of Dublin, which was bound for Caen. When the *Success* got to Mount's Bay at 9.30 on Monday morning the survivors took to their boats again and were towed into Penzance by the schooner *Beryl*. There the injured were treated by surgeons, and the inquest held on Captain Sloan, who was buried in Penzance. The jury recommended that ships laden with coal should always carry a safety lamp. Thomas Smith, a native of Philadelphia who had suffered burns, died three weeks later.

The schooner *Thomas Varcoe*, of Fowey, Stephen Couth master, was bound for Runcorn with china clay. Driven up the Bristol channel by a north-west gale she sank in Lundy roads on 25 October 1870. Captain Couth and his crew of five were rescued by Bristol pilot boat No. 4 and landed at Ilfracombe.

The brig *Mary*, 219 tons register, was owned by Ann Fairchild, of St Mary's, Isles of Scilly. The vessel left Swansea with 315 tons of coal for Bordeaux on 16 December 1870. From Mumbles Head Captain John Day steered south-west by west. The weather was very thick and it was raining. He had the patent log going all the time so that he would have an idea of how far they had travelled. At about 8 pm he went forward to see if the lookout was doing his job, leaving John Shillibeer at the wheel. As he was returning he saw the loom of the land quite close and before he could act, the vessel struck between Rat Island and the south end of Lundy. With the sea making a clean breach over the brig he ordered the boats cleared for launching. The longboat was swamped so they got aboard the punt and made for the north end where they lay until 5.30 am on the 17th when they were picked up by Bristol pilot skiff *Wave*. Richard Chase, master of the *Wave*, intended landing Day and his crew at Padstow but at 1 pm they fell in with the SS *Henry Southam* which was bound from Padstow for Swansea and were landed there at midnight. When passing the *Mary* the steamer's master allowed Day to use the boat to get aboard the wreck but as it was rapidly going to pieces he was unable to save anything. The Board of Trade inquiry concluded that Captain Day was unwise in taking the *Mary* south of Lundy in such poor visibility and suspended his certificate for three months.

The ship *Brenda*, of Halifax, Nova Scotia, was bound for New Orleans with railway track. She left Newport on 7 February 1871 and anchored in Penarth roads because of the poor weather. She left there on the 13th and was towed down channel the tug casting off at 3.10 am on the 14th, the pilot stating that they were north of Lundy as he left. Sail was made but in about half an hour the vessel struck Lundy between Brazen Ward and the Knoll Pins in very hazy conditions. The master, Andrew Webster Mack, and his crew were taken off by a tug and returned to Newport. In the next few months much of the cargo of rails was raised and taken ashore at Bideford and Newport. The hull of the ship was put up for auction at the Royal Hotel, Appledore, on 28 March and bought by Down, Fishwick and Cock of Bideford. The salvage company of Goldfinch of Whitstable, Kent, raised the ship on 2 July and it was towed to Bideford by three steamers. Pearson Adams, one of the divers who had been working on the ship, was killed when struck by the windlass. It was claimed at the time that the *Brenda* was the first Lundy wreck salvaged.

Shortly after four o'clock on the morning of 19 March 1871 the barque *Cornwall*, of Swansea, 487 tons, and the SS *Himalaya*, of West Hartlepool, 682 tons, were in collision in very thick fog about five miles north of Lundy. The barque was bound from Sombrero (a Caribbean island) for Gloucester with a cargo of guano and the steamship from Newport for Reval, Russia, with rails. The *Cornwall* sank within two minutes, drowning her master, Jenkin Jones, the mate, boatswain, carpenter, cook and six seamen. Captain Thomas Whiteman, and crew of the steamer acted very quickly and saved the steward, sailmaker,

> FOR THE BENEFIT OF WHOM IT MAY CONCERN.
>
> MR. HENRY SHEPPARD has been instructed by Messrs. G. W. Jones and Co., Shipbrokers, Newport, to SELL BY AUCTION, at the ROYAL HOTEL, Appledore, on TUESDAY, MARCH 28th, 1871, at Eleven o'clock precisely, subject to conditions then to be read, the HULL, MASTS, and SPARS, of the ship *Brenda*, as she now lies at Lundy Island.
> The *Brenda* registered 958 tons, and was built at Maitland in 1863.
> Auction Offices, 26, Bridge-street, Newport, Mon., March, 18th. 1871. [16.172

Sale of the ship *Brenda* (Monmouthshire Merlin 24 March 1871)

three seamen and the Bristol pilot Joseph Brown. The *Himalaya* remained in the area after daylight but, finding no one else, steamed up channel to dock at Swansea and land the survivors. The Board of Trade inquiry found no one to blame for the collision as the fog had been so thick that neither crew had seen the other's lights.

The 94 ton schooner *Leda*, of and for Nantes, with coal from Cardiff was ten miles south-west of Lundy at 5 am on 28 February 1872 when her master, Ambrose Marie Tascon, was called from below as the lights of an approaching steamer had been seen. The steamer ran into the schooner and cut her down to water level. Tascon and two of his crew got aboard the steamer *Sedgemoor*, Captain Lodge, bound from Middlesbrough to Llanelli with pig iron. Tascon and his two crew then manned a boat with the *Sedgemoor*'s mate and one man to find the other two members of the *Leda*'s crew. By this time the schooner had sunk so they were towed to the spot and found a man in the *Leda*'s boat. The other man, Tascon's brother, had drowned. The *Sedgemoor* docked at Llanelli later that day.

The 272 ton iron-hulled brig *Betsey*, of and from Llanelli, had 450 tons of coal for Cagliari, Sardinia. On 7 May 1872 she was anchored in Lundy roads when at 5.30 am she was struck by the 96 ton brigantine *Ostrich*, of Penzance, which was bound for Plymouth with 158 tons of coal from Porthcawl. A gale had been blowing from west-south-west when it veered to north-west after a squall and the crew of the *Ostrich*, which had been entering the roads to anchor, had lost control. The *Ostrich* lost her bulwarks, stanchions and covering board and sank in ten minutes as her crew got aboard the *Betsey*. Joseph Bailey, the master, was last to leave and as he did so a rope got foul of his leg and dragged him under. He freed his leg and got to the surface. Lines were thrown to him and he was hauled aboard. That afternoon the *Betsey*'s starboard chain parted and, as the port anchor had been damaged in the collision, the master, Edward Samuel, decided to run back and bore up for Mumbles roads where they arrived at 9.30 pm and beached the vessel on the flats off Oystermouth. The *Betsey* was towed into Swansea on the morning of 8 May to repair and land the crew of the *Ostrich*.

The brigantine *Eliza*, of St Ives, Captain Henry David Edwards, loaded a cargo of copper ore at Portreath and left there on 14 March 1873 bound for Pembrey, Carmarthenshire. The next day it blew very hard from the south-east and they put into Hayle to shelter. It was another ten days before the weather settled and they could sail again. Then at 11.45 on the evening of 27 March they were three miles south-east of Lundy when Edwards saw a light a few hundred yards off. He sounded his

> **NOTICE TO MARINERS.**
>
> ENTRANCE TO THE BRISTOL CHANNEL.
>
> TRINITY HOUSE, London, 1st June, 1872.
>
> WRECK IN LUNDY ISLAND ROADS.—Notice is hereby given that a Green Buoy marked 'Wreck,' has been placed about 25 fathoms East from the wreck of a vessel (name unknown) sunk in Lundy Island Roads.
> The Buoy lies in 9 fathoms at low water spring tides, with the following Compass Bearings, viz.:—
>
> North Point of the Island .. .. N by W ½ W
> Rat Island .. .. W by S
> Landing Place .. .. West
>
> The masts of the sunken vessel show about 4 or 5 feet at low water.
> By order, ROBIN ALLEN, Secretary

The buoy probably marked the wreck of the *Ostrich* (*Lloyd's List* 3 June 1872)

foghorn which was answered by a bell but the steamer *Sir Bevis*, of Southampton, bound from Cardiff for Malta with coal, struck the *Eliza* on the port bow and sank her in two minutes. Captain Edwards and the boy, Joshua Behenna, clung to a hatch cover and were picked up by the steamer's boat which then searched for the others but failed to find anyone. Those lost were William Quick Grenfell and Cyrus Blewett of St Ives, James Cloak of Porthcawl and R. Ching of Hayle. The steamer landed Edwards and the boy at St Ives the next morning. The steamer's officers promised £20 to the widows of Grenfell and Blewett and the seamen gave Edwards and the boy £8. A Board of Trade inquiry was held into the loss of the *Eliza* at which Captain Thomas Kemp of the *Sir Bevis* was found fully to blame for having proceeded on the voyage knowing that the steam whistle was defective. His certificate was suspended for six months. The chief engineer was reprimanded as he was responsible for the condition of the whistle.

The Newport pilot cutter *Mary Ann* left port on 21 April 1873. She went as far as ten miles west of Lundy, that being the extent of her master George Morgan's limits. They cruised from there up to Lundy from the 22nd to 27th. On Sunday 27th they were about two miles east-south-east of Lundy when the cutter sprang a leak aft and sank within two hours. Morgan and his crew were picked up from their punt by the Newport cutter *Alarm*. They had lost their clothes and instruments.

The following day another vessel was lost but this was about twenty miles to the north-west of Lundy. The brigantine *Keldhead*, of Aberystwyth, 133 tons, had been built at Traethgwyn, Cardiganshire, in 1862 and was owned by Evan Phillips of New Quay. She left Bone, Algeria, on 27 March 1873 with iron ore for Swansea. Head winds were experienced as far as Cape St Vincent. The weather was not bad across the Bay of Biscay but on 26 April when off Land's End she sprang a leak. All hands worked at the pumps until 2 am on the 28th. The water was then up to the beams and the crew exhausted. Captain Thomas Davies and his crew got aboard the lifeboat with provisions, chronometer, compass and spare clothes. The *Keldhead* sank after half an hour by which time the London ship *Canada* was approaching and picked them up. The *Canada*, bound from Dundee, arrived in Penarth roads and the *Keldhead*'s crew were landed by tug and went straight to Cardiff Sailors' Home.

In May 1873 Thomas Reed, aged twenty, an assistant on pilot Edward Comerford's cutter *Emily* No. 11, went ashore near Lundy's Gannet Stone to gather gulls' eggs but fell from the cliff and was killed.

The weather in the early hours of 23 October 1873 was described as "exceedingly wild, very dark, blowing and raining hard". A number of Bristol pilot cutters were sheltering in Lundy roads when the *Village Belle* No. 37 and *True Blue* No. 4 collided at about 2 am. The *Village Belle* sank straight away, her master William Preston, crew James Hale and James Thomas, taking to the punt having no time to save anything. They were picked up by the *True Blue*, Edward Canby master, and landed at Pill the following day.

The SS *Pallion*, of London, 862 tons, left Cardiff on 4 November 1873 with 1,800 tons of coal for Suez. She was to the west of Lundy at 9.30 am on the 5th when the main shaft broke. The Cardiff tug *Start* took the *Pallion* in tow. After a few hours Captain Griggs hailed the tug to report that the ship was settling. The propeller had moved round the ragged end of the shaft, struck the stern post, and holed the hull. By 2 pm the fires were put out and the crew abandoned and boarded the *Start*. The *Pallion* sank stern first at 6 pm four miles west of Lundy. The tug landed the twenty-five crew at Cardiff the next morning.

On 7 June 1874 the Bristol pilot cutter *Providence* No. 19 was at anchor in Lundy roads when her master, Samuel Buck, realised she was low in the water. Going into the hold he found she was leaking so he and his crew worked at the pumps and used buckets to bail. The water gained on them and, with the vessel fast settling, they launched the punt and got all their clothes and gear aboard. They signalled the tug *Gold Digger* and this came alongside, took them aboard, and landed them at Ilfracombe that evening. Though the cutter was almost fifty years old it was a considerable loss to the crew.

In October 1874 the *North Devon Journal* reported "The *Fanny* of Bideford has passed away at the age of 74 years". This smack was owned and skippered by William Guard of Appledore and sank at the island on one of her regular trips to Lundy for a cargo of granite.

The schooner *Jeanne et Robert*, of Portrieux, Brittany, left Newport for Bordeaux with coal on 15 January 1876. She anchored in Lundy roads with the wind at south-west but at 7.30 am on the 21st the wind veered to north-east and soon a strong gale was blowing. Then it began to snow heavily. The anchor chains parted and the schooner drove ashore and broke up. All hands removed their boots and heavy clothes and attempted to swim ashore. Captain Le Cerf and two of the men were washed back, as the surf rebounded from the beach, and drowned. Four others got ashore. They were the mate Pierre Jean Bodin, and seamen Jean Francois, Pierre Bougnon and Jean Marie Conan. Thomas Ellis, master of Bristol pilot cutter No. 1 was cruising off Lundy and hearing of the wreck went ashore and took the four to Pill. Having landed them they were then taken to the Sailors' Home on The Grove, Bristol, where the French consul arrived to arrange their return home.

The brigantine *Mary Anne*, of Aberystwyth, sailed from Middlesbrough with pig iron for Swansea on 25 July 1876. She put into Newhaven to shelter and left there on the 8th August. On the evening of the 13th she was a few miles to the south-east of Lundy when it was realised that she was leaking. The crew laboured at the pumps but by the early hours of the next day Captain Michael Jones realised she was sinking so ordered his crew to collect all their belongings and take to the boat. They stood by for a few hours and saw it go down bow first about ten miles east-north-east of Lundy at 4 am. There was thick fog but the sea was calm and after twelve hours rowing they landed at Briton Ferry near Neath, Glamorgan.

"The Kingdom of Heaven"

WILLIAM HUDSON HEAVEN *(right)* bought Lundy in 1836 with the intention that it would be a summer resort for his family where he would be able to enjoy the shooting. Heaven was the son of a gentleman and he went to Harrow and Oxford. He was a well-travelled man who inherited estates in Jamaica and became a Freeman of the City of Bristol. When he bought Lundy, it was essentially a farm with a lighthouse and a castle. There was no church, no school, no doctor, no shop, no meeting room.

He built "The Villa" – later renamed Millcombe House – and made major improvements to the Beach Road. Having bought Lundy as a summer retreat, he decided some years later to live permanently on the island. He was a lay reader and he was devoted to his family. The portrait *(below)* by Monanteuil of the Heaven family children in 1832 hangs in Millcombe House. The eldest son, Hudson Grosett Heaven, is on the left. His bookish nature led to him being known in the family as "Phi", short for "Philosopher". He took holy orders and came to teach on Lundy in 1863, where he became the minister of the island. He inherited Lundy on the death of his father in 1883 and realised his ambition to build a church on the island. First he built an iron church which was replaced by the present church of St Helen in 1897. It was consecrated by the Bishop of Exeter who had a rough crossing to reach Lundy; he said that he had no difficulty in believing in the doctrine of Purgatory after what he had experienced to reach the Kingdom of Heaven.

A later child, who doesn't appear in the painting, Amelia Ann Heaven, known as Millie, was sickly and never married but chronicled the family's life on Lundy with wit and invention of language: "Everyone did nothing in particular and the rest looked on". One day, the wind was "ESE and E and then perpendicular". On another occasion, the fog was "like a naked feather bed". Her diaries are a major source of information for the period, including maritime comings and goings – on which the family were totally dependent – and the not infrequent shipwrecks.

As the "lords of the manor" and the best educated people on the island, the Heavens naturally took on the responsibility of dealing with shipwrecked mariners and meeting their medical and other needs until they could be taken to the mainland.

1877-1883: SS *Ethel* wrecked on Lundy's Black Rock

THE steamship *Ethel*, of Newcastle, 810 tons, left Bilbao for Newport with a cargo of iron ore on Saturday 3 February 1877. The ship was wrecked on the Black Rock just off the south-west tip of Lundy on the morning of the 6th. There was just one survivor of the crew of twenty. He was John Lawrence, the first mate, who was landed at Cardiff and told a journalist from the *South Wales Daily News* what had happened: "I have been mate of the ship for two and a half years. We left Bilbao on Saturday morning with iron ore for Newport. We were abreast of Trevose Head at midnight on Monday. The wind then being west-south-west moderate. At 4 am Tuesday the log showed 32 miles from Trevose Head. At half past four I went below leaving the captain and second mate in charge of the deck. At 5.30 I was woken by the ship striking heavily and ran on deck meeting the captain on the poop deck. He told me to get my cork jacket as it was all up with us. The fog was very thick and all I could see was a rock about 200 yards off the starboard bow. I got the jacket and came on deck again and tried to launch the lifeboat by cutting the davit tackle. The lifeboat was washed out of its chocks and thrown against the mainmast and stove in. I, the second mate and four seamen were aboard it. I was thrown out as it struck the mast. When I came to the surface I was overboard but clutching the jacket and ten yards from the poop which was the only part still above water. I saw the captain and engineers on the poop and sung out to them that I was going to make for the shore. We were about a mile and a half from a suitable landing place in smooth water. Some of the crew were struggling in the water close to me. After half an hour I saw the chart house floating and swam towards it. A fireman and seaman were on it. We heard a man shout that he was on the bottom of a lifeboat so the fireman and I swam to him. It was the third engineer. We righted the boat and found it was split at both ends. I stayed there half an hour but in that time the fireman Henry Rothston died. The boat got near the shore so I jumped out. I saw it capsize. I swam round to a small bay and got ashore. I now felt exhausted and very cold. I sat down for about three quarters of an hour hoping that someone would come and help. Getting very stiff I decided to try to scale the cliff as the tide was rising and I was afraid of being drowned. It took me an hour and a half to climb the cliff cutting my feet and hands on the sharp rocks. All I had on was the shirt and pair of drawers that I was wearing in bed. When I got to the top I saw that the sea on the east side was smooth and that two tugs and a smack were anchored there. I hailed one tug and told the master that a ship was sinking on the other side and the crew swimming in their cork jackets. He put to sea and directed me to the house of Lundy's owner Mr Heaven. There I was treated very kindly and given clothes. Mr Heaven's doctor dressed my wounds. The tug searched for three hours but found no one. The *Ethel* had sunk and only the top of the mast was above water. I stayed on the island on Wednesday and was brought up to Cardiff by the tug *Wanderer* on Thursday morning."

The *Ethel* had left the Tyne in January and, after delivering its cargo of coal at St Nazaire, sailed for Bilbao. The crew had signed articles at the Shipping Office in North Shields. They were Captain William Reeves of Sunderland, John Lawrence, mate, of Heworth on Tyne, R. Jefferson, second mate, of Whitby, Edward Fisk, carpenter, of Yarmouth, James Murray, cook, of Glasgow, William Bowman, boatswain, of Montrose, able-seamen William Poston of Shrewsbury, James McMillan of Aberdeen, Charles Smith of Heligoland, G. Stannard of London, David Petersen from Sweden, first engineer Edward Hails of Newcastle, second engineer William Pellet of London, third engineer Thomas Beard of Southampton, donkeyman M. Turner of Gateshead, firemen H. Rothston of Grimsby, James Fox of Jarrow, Lawrence Blessington also of Jarrow and William Reed of South Shields. The steward did not sign on at Shields and perhaps was taken on in Spain. Lawrence described him as "a foreigner".

On Friday 9 February the Cardiff pilot cutter No. 50, John Lark Hervey master, found a body wearing a cork life jacket about eight miles south-east of Lundy and landed it at Ilfracombe. The police found a silver watch in one pocket retailed by E. Wakefield and Son of Gateshead. Around the man's neck was a medallion of the Shipwrecked Mariners' Society with the membership number 26,763 scratched on. This identified him as Edward Hails of Newcastle, chief engineer of the *Ethel*. His widow and brother-in-law attended the inquest held at Ilfracombe. A week or so later another body was found also in a life jacket. There were three Spanish coins and a farthing in one pocket and a boatswain's call in the other. This may have been William Bowman. The *Ethel*'s bell, recovered by divers in 1982, is on display in Lundy's Marisco Tavern.

Medallion worn by members of the Shipwrecked Mariners' Society

Obverse (left): Bust of Vice-Admiral Horatio Nelson. Legend: "ENGLAND EXPECTS EVERY MAN WILL DO HIS DUTY".

Reverse (right): Port-quarter view of a three-masted ship partially dismasted driving onto rocks. Legend: "SHIPWRECKED MARINERS SOCIETY. 1857".

Issued annually as receipt for subscriptions. Pierced with hole for suspension. Space for membership number to be scratched on the obverse

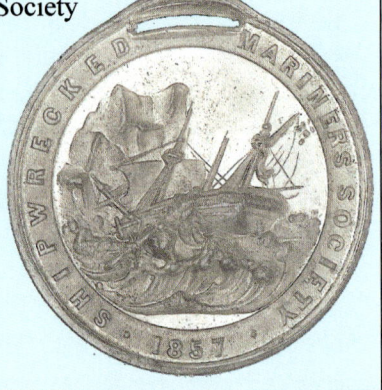

At 2 am on 12 August 1877 the Newport cutter *Alarm* was putting pilot William Watts aboard the SS *Pelaw*, of London, two miles east of Lundy. The steamer struck and sank the *Alarm*. Watts and his two crew were picked up. Two weeks later the 447 ton barque *Arturo*, of Genoa, with iron ore from Portman Bay, Spain, for Cardiff hit a rock at the south end of Lundy. In danger of sinking, she was towed by the tug *Refuge* to Ilfracombe. Having been pumped out and repaired she was towed to Cardiff to discharge the ore and put up for sale at the West Bute dock on 22 October.

The dandy *Swift* sailed from Swansea on 11 October 1877 bound for Hull with a cargo of copperas which was insured for £225. ("Dandy" refers to the type of rigging, but the exact definition varies.) She made slow progress down channel due to the deteriorating weather. A south-west gale blew for two days from the morning of the 15th and the *Swift* sank to the north-east of Lundy on the 16th. Captain Guy and the two crew were picked up and landed at Swansea the next day.

At 1.30 am on 17 May 1878 the American schooner *H.R. Tilton*, 479 tons, bound from Le Havre for Cardiff, collided with a small vessel south-east of Lundy. Some of the schooner's crew wanted to launch their boat to search for the men that were heard calling for help but the master sailed on. It was some days before it was realised that the pilot cutter *Pride of the Taff*, of Cardiff, was lost with her master Evan Jones aged 47, his nephew Thomas Jones, 20, and John Duggan, 17. The nameboard of the cutter was found washed up at Newton Pool, Porthcawl. A case was held at Cardiff county court against the owners of the *H.R. Tilton* for the value of the cutter. The nautical assessors considered that the schooner was wholly to blame and ordered £400 to be paid into court. Evan Jones was both master and half owner of the cutter. He left a widow and three children.

The fog guns on Lundy's west coast were replaced by rockets from 1 August 1878. They exploded at a height of about 600 feet and when required were fired every ten minutes.

The SS *G.N. Wilkinson*, of Southampton, was of 475 tons register. When the vessel arrived at Dieppe from Newport in November 1878, her master W. Hodgson made the following report: "On Friday 8 November at 4 am there was a strong north-west gale with a heavy sea. I eased the ship off Trevose Head, the sea making a clean breach over us. At 7.30 am sighted a schooner flying distress signals. At 9 am ran up alongside and found her to be sinking. Hove a line aboard but to no purpose. Kept by her and made several attempts to take the crew off, all in vain, sea running so heavily it was impossible to launch a boat. At 2.45 pm ran alongside with great risk for the last time. As she was foundering her crew jumped overboard. Saved the captain and one man with our lifebuoys, the other two taken down. Steamed around the wreck but they never rose again. Lundy bore north-east about 14 or 15 miles. Steamed back to Lundy and on Saturday 9 November put the two survivors on board No. 5 pilot cutter of Falmouth to be landed". The schooner was the *Heligan*, of Truro, bound from Cardiff for Gweek, with coal. The steamer had rescued her master R. Richards and seaman S. Hughes. The mate and boy had drowned.

The SS *Ralph Creyke*, of Goole, left Cardiff at 5 pm on Wednesday 19 February 1879 with 750 tons of coal for Dieppe. At four o'clock the next morning the north-west wind was approaching gale force. The ship was then about ten miles south-west of Lundy and labouring heavily. The engineers noticed that the vessel was leaking. The donkey engine was started and all the pumps working but the water gained on them. All hands were called on deck with the ship slowly sinking. The two lifeboats were launched. George Moore, second engineer, got into the port lifeboat with seven others, Captain Ellwood and seven men into the starboard boat. The ship foundered about half an hour later. The two lifeboats remained close and were making for Lundy with a heavy sea against them. Between ten and eleven am the master's boat was seen to fill with water. The other boat made for it but was almost swamped and had to abandon the attempt. Later two men were washed out of the flooded port boat and the master's boat drifted away. At about one o'clock that afternoon the steamer *Charles Goddard* spotted the port lifeboat and picked up Moore, the steward, two stokers and two seamen and landed them at Cardiff. The starboard boat which had contained the master and seven men was found derelict and full of water near Lundy and taken into Ilfracombe on Saturday afternoon. Some days later a telegram was received from Lloyd's agent at Nantes saying that the SS *Cambronne*, of Nantes, which had been bound from Cardiff for St Nazaire, had found the starboard boat with just George Cannon, second mate, and Edward Bonnett, seaman, alive. The other six had died of exposure. The two were taken aboard. The *Cambronne* continued her passage and landed the men at St Nazaire. They returned to Britain in the SS *Langley* which landed them at Sunderland.

The 45 ton smack *Lady Louise* was bound from Waterford to Bideford when the ballast shifted in the rough weather and the pumps were choked. The master and mate failed to right the vessel and took to the boat to the west of Lundy on 10 October 1880. The crew of the German barque *Empress*, which was bound to Penarth with railway sleepers, spotted them and they were picked up. The barque's master, Captain Vehlow, was awarded a pair of binoculars by the Board of Trade.

Between eight and nine on the morning of 16 November 1880 Bristol pilot cutter No. 5 was between Hartland Point and Lundy. Pilot A. Cheswell and a member of the crew were below eating breakfast when gale force winds struck and swept Thomas Adams aged twenty-three and Joseph Parfitt aged seventeen overboard where they drowned.

At midnight on 8 December 1880 the barque *Amazon*, of Grimstadt (Norway), which was bound from Cardiff for Pernambuco (Brazil), collided with the Cardiff steam tug *Rattler* to the north of Lundy. The tug crew boarded the *Amazon* which put back and docked at Cardiff for repairs to her bows. The next day a ship reported the *Rattler* floating "bows under" near the Helwick lightship, off Gower.

The Norwegian barque *Athlet*, 780 tons, was bound from Cardiff to Algoa Bay (South Africa). She passed Lundy at about 6 pm on 29 October 1881 and a few hours later, when twenty miles west of the island, Captain Petersen saw smoke billowing out of the after hatch. The coal cargo was on fire. The vessel turned back for Lundy and met the Pill pilot cutter *Emma* No. 25, Edward Rowland master, which stood by. Hoping to stifle the flames the ventilators were closed but the cargo exploded and blew off a section of the deck. The crew took to the boats and were taken aboard the *Emma* which landed them at Appledore. The Norwegian vice-consul sent them to London from where they got a passage home.

The brigantine *Marco Polo*, of Cork, was sailing up channel in ballast when her steering gear was badly damaged in a gale on Monday 19 December 1881. Captain Jeremiah Falvey hoisted a distress signal. The next day the Cork steamer *Minna* approached. The *Minna* kept close to the *Marco Polo* but the sea conditions were so bad that it was impossible to launch the boat. Captain John Leyne ran the steamer alongside the brigantine, which was now sinking about twelve miles north-west of Lundy and, with the aid of lines, got the four men of the *Marco Polo* aboard and landed them at Newport on Wednesday morning.

The barque *Paola Revello*, of Genoa, ran ashore near the granite quarries in thick fog late on the evening of 31 August 1882. She had left Cardiff for Cape Town with 887 tons of coal. *The Western Morning News* reported that Alfred Ray, a Bristol pilot, went alongside but the barque's crew drew their knives on him. Ray was a Freemason and was said to have made the right signs to Captain Revello who allowed him aboard. The vessel was got off and anchored in the roads but was then found to be sinking. The tug *Tweed* was called in and beached the vessel at the landing place for £20. Ray sailed to Ilfracombe and informed Huxtable, Lloyd's agent, who sent telegrams to the Italian consul and the ship's brokers at Cardiff. The ship was advertised for sale by auction on 15 September but appears to have been sold privately to a group at Bideford. It was then taken to Westacott's graving dock at Appledore for repair. Captain B. Revello, who owned the barque with his brother, expressed his gratitude to William Hudson Heaven, Lundy's owner, for his kindness to him and his crew.

Auction of the barque *Paola Revello*
(*Bristol Mercury* 14 September 1882)

> PORT OF CARDIFF.
> FOR THE BENEFIT OF WHOM IT MAY CONCERN.
> MESSRS. SHORT & DUNN are Instructed to SELL by PUBLIC AUCTION, on FRIDAY Next, 15th of September, at the CHAMBER OF COMMERCE, CARDIFF (unless previously disposed of by Private Contract, of which due notice will be given),
> The Barque "PAOLA REVELLO," of Genoa, Now lying stranded on the Beach on the east side of Lundy Island, 547 tons net register, and carrying about 900 tons, built of oak in 1871, copper fastened, and was re-metalled in 1881.
> Also, the Sails, Ropes, Anchors, Chains, Materials, and Stores, removed from the Ship and landed on Lundy Island.
> The Sale will take place at 11 a.m.
> Immediately afterwards the CARGO of 887 Tons of Nixon's Navigation Smokeless Steam COAL will be Sold.
> For further particulars apply to F. SCHIAFFINO, Esq., Messrs Nixon's Navigation Coal Company (Limited); or to the Auctioneers, Bute Docks, Cardiff. 8192

The SS *Cambronne*, of Nantes, which had picked up two men from the *Ralph Creyke* in 1879, was herself sunk in 1882. On Sunday 26 November 1882 she was bound from Cardiff to Rouen with coal. A strong gale was blowing from the north-west that evening and she sought shelter in Lundy roads when the London steamer *Marion* collided with her. The French vessel was badly holed below the waterline and was sinking fast. Captain Sauzereau threw the cabin boy, Douvan, onto the *Marion* and he and the mate Jean Maurice followed. The Greek fireman seized a lifebuoy, jumped into the sea and was picked up by a tug. The rest of the crew, fourteen men, were drowned. The *Marion*'s bows were holed so she returned to Swansea where she had loaded coal for Copenhagen.

The barque *Storjohann*, of Tvedestrand, Norway, was bound from Bordeaux for Cardiff with a cargo of pitprops when she was in collision with the SS *Pelaw* about five miles south-east of Lundy after dark on 13 December 1882. Nicholas Guthrie, master of the *Pelaw* which was bound for London with coal, ordered the lifeboat launched and it returned an hour later with all hands of the barque which was holed but kept afloat by the cargo. The next day the *Pelaw* steamed to Morte Bay and put the rescued crew aboard a Bristol pilot cutter. They then moved to the SS *Gironde* which landed them at Cardiff. The derelict *Storjohann* drifted down channel and was eventually found off Strumble Head, Pembrokeshire, and towed into Milford Haven.

The barquentine *Heroine*, 389 tons, left Newport with 700 tons of iron and coal for Rosario (Argentina) at 9.20 on the morning of 13 December 1882. She was towed down channel by the tug *Susan Gibbs* which cast off abreast the Foreland at mid-day. Captain James Kirby then steered west-north-west till 7 pm, the wind being a fresh breeze from east-north-east, the sea smooth. The course was changed to west by north until 8 pm and then to west. The night was very dark and hazy. At 11.30 pm the vessel struck the north-west point of Lundy. The sails were backed but the vessel failed to get off. All hands abandoned in the boat and got ashore on the island. With the hold flooded, the vessel swung round and sank in eight fathoms. Captain Kirby and his crew were landed at Cardiff on 17 December. The Board of Trade inquiry found James Kirby guilty of careless navigation and suspended his certificate for three months. A year earlier he had rescued the crew of a French vessel which had foundered off Bermuda. The French merchant marine had presented him with a binocular glass.

The barque *Burnswark* bound for Old Calabar, Nigeria, with a general cargo left Bristol at 8.30 am on 13 December 1882. That afternoon the vessel ran ashore on the east side of Lundy near the Quarter Wall in very thick fog. On the flood tide the ship began to bump heavily on the rocks so Captain William Henry Luke and the twelve hands abandoned and were landed at Ilfracombe by Bristol pilot cutter No. 22, Joseph Thayer master. Part of the cargo was landed at Appledore and auctioned there with the hull which still lay at Lundy a month later. In the same week, the brigantine *Albrecht*, Rio Grande (Brazil) to Bridgwater with hides, stranded on Lundy. Though leaking badly her crew kept her afloat by continuous effort at the pumps. She was towed to Penarth roads by the Cardiff steamer *Ingoldsby* which was bound home from Antwerp in ballast.

The brig *Zoodochos Pighi*, 235 tons, of Skopelos, Greece, sailed from Penarth with a cargo of 466 tons of coal at 8 am on 6 December 1883 bound for Buenos Aires. Her master Nintis Georgara reported: "At 4.30 pm tide half flood, the weather fine, wind north-west strong with a heavy sea. Ship was then about 10 miles north-east of Lundy. Pumped ship and found she was making water. 5.30 pm she became unmanageable so we bore away for Lundy. At 7 pm in a sinking condition about 13 miles north of Lundy. We left in two boats and pulled towards Lundy". They were unable to find a landing place but at 10 pm saw a light and rowed towards it. It was the tug *Trevose*, of Cardiff. Captain Georgara and his seven crew were taken aboard and landed at Ilfracombe at 11 am the next day.

1884-1885: A young lad the only survivor

THE SS *Hornet*, of Glasgow, John Tomlin a native of Fowey was her master, left Newport on 24 January 1884 with 622 tons of coal for Marseilles and had 131 tons in her bunkers. She got as far as the Isles of Scilly but was driven back up channel by a strong gale. On the 27th George Bayley, master of the SS *Bowesfield*, of Stockton, which was bound from Cardiff to Malta, saw the *Hornet* near Lundy drifting up channel flying her ensign "jack downwards" as a signal of distress. The *Bowesfield* steered for the *Hornet* but as she got near, two seas swept over the ship and it sank stern first. Four men were then seen on floating wreckage. Captain Bayley got his ship near and two of his crew went over the side on lines and attempted to catch the men as they were swept by. They saved Joseph Ellery of Polruan, Cornwall, and got him aboard and put him straight in a berth to recover. The *Bowesfield* cruised about but was unable to find anyone else. Ellery was just fourteen years old. He had recovered in a few hours and told his rescuers the name of his vessel and its destination. The *Bowesfield* ran up channel to find a pilot boat to take the lad ashore. Having got as far as Breaksea, on the Glamorgan coast, and not finding one and the gale increasing and the weather thick with hail he put the ship's head round and proceeded on his voyage to Malta.

Seventeen men had drowned when the *Hornet* sank. The Board of Trade inquiry concluded that the ship was in a good and seaworthy condition when she left Newport and that her loss was probably due to someone on board having unintentionally opened the seacock which allowed water to flow in and flood the vessel. Captain George Bayley was awarded the silver medal of the Board of Trade and this was presented to him at their Newport office in May 1884.

The barque *Eurydice*, of and for St John's, New Brunswick, had left Liverpool with a cargo of coal and salt. After leaving St George's Channel, a gale drove her east and on the afternoon of 10 February 1884 she was about twenty five miles north-west of Lundy when a schooner was seen flying distress signals. Captain John Kilgallan of the *Eurydice* waited for the schooner to drift towards him. Captain Fishley, master of the schooner, hailed him and said she was leaking badly and sinking. She was the *Little Racer*, of Padstow, bound from Plymouth for Cork with a cargo of 124 tons of bagged manure. One of his crew had died of exposure because of the fearful weather since leaving port. Captain Kilgallan offered his crew £1 each if they would volunteer to launch a boat and rescue the schooner's crew. Four men volunteered and launched the boat but with the sea running so high they could not get near and returned to the barque. As soon as it got dark, lights were burnt on the barque to show her position and at 11.30 the schooner got under the barque's quarter and the mate Francis Lark, of Port Isaac, jumped and caught hold of the barque's chain plates. The barque's steward went over the side and got a line round Lark's waist and he was hauled aboard. Captain Fishley followed but missed his hold fell into the sea and was drowned. Lines were thrown to the boy, Thomas Tucker, who was still aboard. He caught one but was so weak he was unable to hold it. A huge sea broke over the schooner, the vessels separated, and in a few minutes she sank. The weather was so bad that the *Eurydice* was driven right up channel to Newport where Francis Lark was landed. The following month John Kilgallan was awarded the silver medal of the Board of Trade.

Three ships are said to have run ashore on the east side of Lundy in thick fog on the morning of 27 June 1884 though only two were named. The SS *Wimbledon*, of London, which was bound from Penarth for Madeira, did so at 2.20 and the SS *Baines Hawkins*, of Newcastle, bound from Cardiff for Antwerp, at 2.45. Both vessels got off and docked at Swansea, their fore compartments being flooded. A court of inquiry was held and learnt that neither crew had seen or heard the rockets which were fired every ten minutes from the west side of the island. "It is the intention of the court to make a representation to the authorities with regard to the inadequate signalling arrangements at Lundy".

Edited extract from the *Weekly Mail* (Cardiff), 2 August 1884

Many steamers anchored in Lundy roads on 18 December 1884 seeking shelter from a north-west gale. The SS *William Banks*, of London, Captain Langlois, had left Cardiff at eight that morning and anchored close inshore at 8 pm. An hour later the SS *Vagliano Brothers* anchored further out. With the gale increasing this ship moved closer to the island and struck the *William Banks* causing serious damage to the ship's forecastle. The *William Banks* returned to Cardiff and was repaired at Roath Dock.

The SS *Peer of the Realm*, of Newcastle, 1,182 tons, left Cardiff with 2,530 tons of coal for Bombay at 3.30 pm on 11 February 1885. As she steamed down channel, dense fog set in and the speed was reduced. The lead was used but the ship struck near the Knoll Pins on Lundy's east coast. The crew got ashore and left for Cardiff, leaving the mate, chief engineer, donkeyman and carpenter to assist the salvors. An attempt to float the ship was made on 28 March but this failed. A month or so later the underwriters decided to abandon efforts to save the ship and it was put up for auction on 16 July and knocked down for £300 to J.M. Gunn & Co. of Cardiff. The Mount Stuart Graving Dock Co. was called in and their manager, T.W. Wailes, took a team to Lundy aboard the salvage vessel *Hoy Head*. They floated the *Peer of the Realm* and the ship was towed to Cardiff by the tugs *Noord*, *Falcon*, *Briton* and *Levant* on 14 August. A Board of Trade inquiry had been held at which John Morgan, the senior man at the signal station, had said that with the fog rockets being fired from the west side of the island it was highly unlikely that they would be heard from the ship. Also with the fog being so thick they would not have been seen nor would the lights of the lighthouse. The court thought that the lead should have been used more often but though Captain Edwin Knowles was in default they did not suspend his certificate.

The Brixham schooner *Hirondelle* had left Cardiff with a cargo of coal for Dakar, West Africa. At 4.30 on the morning of Friday 20 March 1885 she was in collision, three miles north-east of Lundy, with the barquentine *Mary Ann*, of Newport, which was also outward bound. Captain Henry Cove and his crew of seven scrambled aboard their boat and boarded the *Mary Ann* to watch as the *Hirondelle* sank in five or six minutes. The *Mary Ann* returned up channel and landed Cove and his crew at Cardiff before docking at Newport for repairs to her bows and headgear.

> **THE DANGERS OF LUNDY ISLAND.**
>
> THE BOARD OF TRADE INQUIRY AT SWANSEA.
>
> REPRESENTATION BY THE COURT.
>
> The Board of Trade inquiry into the stranding of the Baines Hawkins on Lundy Island last month was concluded at Swansea on Monday
>
> . . .
>
> The Great Beacon at Lundy, which was very useful at times, might, on the morning of the 27th, as well have been in America. The island was narrow and lofty, and there were often thick fogs obscuring it. The fog signals were only used on the western side of the island, and as they were not used till 3.40 that morning were of no use. The fog signalman, although admitting that there might be fog on the eastern side and not on the western side, and *vice versâ*, said he had no duty on the eastern side, and though he had lived for ten years on the island he would not, or could not, tell what its breadth was. The Court begged leave to point out that the provision made years ago for averting danger on the western side should now be extended to the eastern side of the island also.

1886-1888: The great gale of October 1886

THE *North Devon Journal* of Thursday 28 October 1886 carried the following item: "Lundy The Great Gale. A Lundy island correspondent wrote us, under date October 18th. Thursday, Friday and Saturday were terrible days here. It was one of the heaviest gales ever known, sweeping the island with terrific force. Nothing like it has occurred for years. Several ships in distress passed by, notably the *Inversnaid*, a full-rigged vessel, 2,600 tons, from Cardiff. She narrowly escaped going ashore on the Hen and Chickens reef. Her canvas was blown to ribbons and with a heavy list to starboard she appeared unmanageable. The seas broke over her with tremendous force. It is feared that she has foundered or gone ashore on the Cornish coast. With the many wrecks occurring in this neighbourhood, it will be a surprise to you to learn that we have no means for life saving provided. Surely we ought to have a rocket apparatus. Twenty large steamers, beside the 'smaller fry', successfully rode out the gale here. The Government ought to take steps to improve the natural harbour for the Channel, but at present it's all 'talk-talk-talk'. Sooner or later a terrible disaster will open their eyes to their short-sightedness and supine-ness."

The storm of 15-17 October 1886 was described as "one of the most severe hurricanes that has visited these coasts for a very considerable time". Many sailing ships were driven ashore on the Glamorgan coast and in Carmarthen Bay. But it is the four vessels which were lost near Lundy – the *Boswedden*, *Inversnaid*, *Juanita* and *Henry* – which concern us here.

The schooner *Boswedden*, of Penzance, was bound home from Briton Ferry with 253 tons of coal. Her master was John Dusting, the mate his nephew also John Dusting. Henry Trewhella, David James, the boy Thomas Bailey, and two men from Middlesbrough were the crew. Two young men, Henry Tucker and John Carne, were passengers returning to Penzance. Some weeks earlier the schooner had been at Littlehampton where two of her usual hands, Edward Richards and William Jewell, had been involved in a disturbance at a public house and were jailed. The two Middlesbrough men were signed on as replacements. The schooner left Briton Ferry at 8 am on Thursday 14 October. She was last reported leaving Lundy roads by the ship *Vendome*. A few days later wreckage and a bucket marked *Boswedden* were found at Lundy. The Board of Trade inquiry into the loss of the schooner, which was held at Swansea, heard that she sailed with a freeboard measuring 18 inches which was 6 inches too little. It found there was a strong possibility that the vessel had been overwhelmed by the dangerous seas of the violent gale of the 15th and foundered with all hands.

The ship *Inversnaid*, of Liverpool, 1,613 tons, left Penarth at 7 am 14 October with a cargo of 2,316 tons of coal bound for Singapore. She was towed down channel by the tug *Brilliant Star* which cast off about fifteen miles west of Lundy at 11.30 pm. At about 9.30 am on the 16th the tug *Flying Fox* saw the *Inversnaid* two miles off the north end of Lundy. She appeared to be heading for the roads. The ship was unable to weather the north of the island so ran down the west coast as the *Flying Fox* steamed down the east coast. At about 10.30 Rowlands, a Bristol pilot, saw the ship running down the west coast under two upper topsails and fore-top staysail. She was labouring heavily apparently in distress, her lower topsails, main staysail and jib blown away. She had a strong list to starboard. When the *Flying Fox* reached the south end of Lundy the ship was seen running south or south-south-west before the wind which was blowing force ten or more from the north. The tug steamed close to the ship's port quarter and her master hailed Captain John Dodds and advised him to seek shelter under the lee of the island. The ship had a heavy list and a spar was over the starboard side. A heavy rain squall then blew in and when it cleared the ship was nowhere to be seen. The *Flying Fox* steamed around the area for an hour but, finding nothing, left for Cardiff. A few days later parts of the ship were found on the Hen and Chickens rocks off the north-west end of the island. Other wreckage was found on the Devon coast and part of the transom of one of the ship's boats at Port Eynon on the Gower coast. At the Board of Trade inquiry evidence was heard which convinced the court that the cargo had not been fully trimmed at Penarth.

The barque *Juanita*, of North Shields, is often listed as a Lundy wreck but there is little evidence as to where she sank. She sailed from Troon, on the Ayrshire coast, Scotland, on 2 October 1886 with a cargo of coal for Demerara (now Guyana). Some of her wreckage was found near Bideford. Then on 4 November a body was found at Ram's Grove near Rhosili on the Gower coast. It was dressed in yellow oilskin leggings, Wellington boots, blue and white striped stockings with W.T. at the top, tweed trousers, grey Welsh flannel shirt and a red woollen cravat. Reading this report in the *South Wales Daily News*, Rev. J.W. Maurice, the Baptist minister at Dinas Cross, Pembrokeshire, went to Rhosili and identified the body as that of William Thomas, master of the *Juanita*. The body was taken to Dinas Cross for burial. Captain Thomas's son David had also been a member of the crew.

Bristol pilot cutter *Henry* No. 32 had foundered to the west of Lundy in the storm of Friday 15 October. Pilot William Russell and his crew were rescued by the SS *Glenbervie* and transferred to the Cardiff tug *Thomas Collingdon* which landed them at Ilfracombe.

At three o'clock on the morning of Friday 4 March 1887 there was a collision between the SS *Glenmavis*, of Leith, bound from Le Havre for Cardiff and the brigantine *Rosario* bound from Cardiff to Alcudia, Majorca. The collision occurred in poor visibility about five miles south-west of Lundy. After the collision the steamer searched for a couple of hours but, failing to find the brigantine, steamed for Penarth roads. The *South Wales Daily News* of 10 March carried a letter from Manuel Fernandez Luces, master of the *Rosario*, expressing his thanks to the captain, officers and men of the French steamship *Boucan* for having towed his vessel for some hours when in a sinking condition and for taking them on board when they were compelled to abandon. The *Boucan* had landed them at Newport.

The SS *Elsie*, of Whitby, 1,574 tons, left Cardiff with 2,230 tons of coal for St Vincent, Cape Verde islands. Initially Captain Christopher Thompson had intended to pass to the south of Lundy but as the visibility was poor he changed course to pass north of the island. At 5 pm on Friday 20 January 1888 the *Elsie* struck Gannet Rock. With the port bilge on the rock the ship listed to starboard so Thompson ordered the crew away in the boats. They got ashore on the rocks where they spent the night before climbing the cliff at daylight. M.W. Aisbitt, marine surveyor to the underwriters, arrived from Cardiff and salvage began. A third of the cargo was jettisoned and the bow section made watertight. Soon after mid-day on Tuesday 24th the vessel floated at high water and was towed to Cardiff by the tugs *Galloper* and *Empress of India.* The Board of Trade inquiry found Captain Thompson in default for not having used the lead and steaming at too high a speed in the fog. His certificate was suspended for three months. They would have suspended it for longer "but for his long service and general good conduct". A number of mariners and those living on the island complained that the fog gun was often not heard and the lighthouse not seen in fog.

The north-easterly wind was blowing hard and heavy snow was falling in the early hours of 14 February 1888 when the Bristol pilot boat *New Prosperous* was driven ashore near Lundy's landing place and wrecked. Her master William Hunt and his crew were rescued by the steam trawler *Express*, of Milford, and transferred to another Bristol cutter.

1888-1896: Just one survivor of the *City of Exeter*

On Monday 12 March 1888 Lloyd's reported: "The *Sarah Ann* anchored off Lundy. Master reports on Sunday morning Trevose Head bearing east-south-east about 8 miles saw *City of Exeter*, steamer of Exeter, Penarth for St Nazaire, firing signals of distress. Bore up when she signalled 'Will you take me in tow?'. While getting ready she signalled again 'We are leaking and boats stove.' Commenced to get our lifeboat out but, before succeeding, saw vessel roll over and sink. Managed to save one seaman whom we landed at Lundy." The steamer *Sarah Ann* had left Cardiff for Malta on Saturday. Having landed the survivor on Lundy the *Sarah Ann* proceeded on her passage to Malta from where her master, Captain C.A. Todd, sent a statement to the Board of Trade describing what had happened. Simonsen, the survivor, was landed at Appledore by the skiff *Gannet* on 15 March.

The *City of Exeter* was built at Stockton on Tees in 1870. She was of 1,054 tons gross, 787 tons net, and had been a regular trader from the coal ports of South Wales to French and Spanish ports returning with iron ore from Bilbao. The ship left Penarth at 5.30 on the morning of 10 March and steamed to a point off Barry where the pilot left. The sole survivor was able seaman Ole Simonsen, a Norwegian, who described what had happened with the aid of an interpreter. He had gone on watch at 4 am on the 11th. The wind was blowing hard and the sea running high. At about 6 am a heavy sea struck the ship and carried away the wheel chains. The ship's bows swung to starboard and she took the whole force of wind and sea on her port side. The cargo shifted and she listed heavily to starboard and lay in a trough of the sea with the rail and a part of the main hatch under water. Two lifeboats on the starboard side and the gig on port side were carried away. Tackles were connected to the tiller and the rudder kept steady but the ship would not steer due to the heavy list. The crew's attempt at securing tarpaulins over the hatches failed and by 2 pm the engineer reported the water was gaining on the pumps. The engines stopped at about 3 pm. The ship suddenly sank. A lifeboat capsized and Simonsen, two seamen and the mate clung to it. He saw two others holding on to a cork fender, another two on a hatch cover and Captain Popham swimming. The *Sarah Ann* bore down and Simonsen was able to take hold of a line that she lowered and was rescued. The conditions were so bad, it was probably blowing force 10, that the *Sarah Ann* had been unable to launch a lifeboat.

Charles Wilson, principal officer for the London district of the Board of Trade, investigated the tragedy in which the master and fifteen crew had died. The statements of the builders, and owners of the ship, and the trimmers of the cargo showed that she was seaworthy when leaving Penarth. Wilson was surprised to learn that Simonsen stated that the hatches had been bulged out and forced off by the cargo shifting. He had never heard of that happening but thought that it may have accounted for many missing coal laden vessels.

Dense fog on the 8th and 9th of May 1888 caused three vessels to run ashore on Lundy. Richard Thomas, master of the 12 ton paddle tug *Electric*, of Newport, recorded in his deposition that they had left Newport at 4.30 am towing a ship down channel. They cast off at 9.30 pm when five miles west of the island and turned back up channel. At 11.35 pm it was low water, the fog dense and wind west with a moderate breeze. Thomas was on the bridge with the mate at the wheel. Believing the tug was near the island the engine was eased to dead slow and seeing breakers ahead he ordered full speed astern but she struck at the foot of the cliff. The tug was soon sinking and seeing no chance of saving her he ordered out the boat and they abandoned. They lost everything.

Richard Thomas did admit to not having used the lead as they approached Lundy. The fog signal had been heard when they were well to the west of the island but they did not hear it again until the tug had struck. They drifted about in the boat until seven the next morning when they landed on the island. They boarded the tug *Prairie Flower* which landed them at Ilfracombe at 5 pm.

> WRECKED TUG BOAT FOR SALE.
> MESSRS SHORT and DUNN are instructed to SELL by PUBLIC AUCTION, on MONDAY NEXT, 14th May, 1888, at 1 p.m., at the Exchange, Mount Stuart square, Cardiff, the
> PADDLE TUG BOAT ELECTRIC,
> of Newport, as she lies stranded at Lundy Island.
> Engined by Rennoldson, and had new boiler two years ago.
> For further particulars apply to the Auctioneers, Bute Docks, Cardiff.

Auction of the tug *Electric* (*South Wales Daily News* 12 May 1888)

The SS *Radnor*, 1,256 tons gross, of and from Cardiff for Galatz (Galati, Romania) with a cargo of coal, ran ashore near Gull Rock in the fog at about 1.30 on the morning of Wednesday 9 May. Much of the cargo was discharged and the ship pumped dry. She was refloated on 15 May and returned to Cardiff for repair.

The third ship to go ashore in that fog was the SS *Boucan*, of La Rochelle, a regular trader to Cardiff. Her bows were stove in but she was got off and returned to Cardiff with her fore compartment flooded.

At 2.15 on the morning of 5 June 1888 the barque *Tweedsdale* bound down channel struck and sank the steam trawler *City of Gloucester*, of Cardiff, which was fishing so not able to give way to sail. The trawler sank north of Lundy and the barque picked up the crew of seven. The *Tweedsdale* was bound for Genoa but had orders to call at Queenstown (Cobh, Ireland). The trawler's crew transferred to the Liverpool tug *Rattler* which landed them at Dunmore East. Edward Jacob, honorary agent to the Shipwrecked Mariners' Society at Waterford, arranged a passage for them to return to Cardiff.

The ship *South Australian*, of Belfast, 1,039 tons, Captain James Arthurs, left Cardiff at 4 pm on Tuesday 12 February 1889 for Rosario, Argentina, with 5,380 steel rails and 1,067 bundles of fish plates. The tug *Flying Swallow* towed the ship down channel and cast off seven miles north of Lundy at 2.40 on Wednesday morning. A strong gale then came in from south-west. A heavy sea broke over the bows carrying away the port rail and breaking down the deck house. At 4 pm the ship was about ten miles west-north-west of Lundy. It was decided to put back for Penarth roads. It was then realised that some of the rails had shifted and knocked out the starboard cargo port allowing water to pour into the hold. The vessel was sinking so the crew and the master's wife abandoned at about 1 am on Thursday and boarded the lifeboat. As they pulled away it was realised that two men were still on board. The man who had been at the wheel jumped into the sea and was picked up but the black cook remained on board and was lost. The lifeboat drifted east. A quilt was used as a sail. At mid-day the schooner *Spray*, of Wexford, took them aboard off the Gower coast and transferred them to the steam trawler *Flying Scotsman*, of Milford, which landed them at Swansea. The Board of Trade inquiry found that neither the master nor his officers were at fault.

On Thursday 19 December 1889 the master of the steam tug *Norah* reported having picked up a ship's boat marked *Eliza Jones* and a hatch cover about five miles north-east of Lundy at 1 pm on the 17th. The schooner *Eliza Jones*, of Caernarfon, had left Hayle for Bristol but did not arrive. It was presumed that the vessel had sunk and her crew of three drowned. At the same time, parts of a small vessel were seen on the Rattles on Lundy's south end.

At 1.30 on the morning of 19 February 1890 the SS *Highgate*, 927 tons, of Whitby, bound from Mostyn, Flintshire, to Cardiff in ballast, collided with the ship *Sovereign*, 1,193 tons, of Halifax, Nova Scotia, which was bound from Cardiff for Montevideo. The vessels were about ten miles north-east of Lundy. The collision ripped a large hole in the steamer's plates and smashed one of her lifeboats. Realising the steamer was sinking Captain H.C. Lewer ordered the boats away and his crew were joined by three men of the *Sovereign* who had jumped aboard. Six men, including one from the *Sovereign*, who had got aboard the jolly boat were not seen again. A second boat with the *Highgate*'s mates and seven crew was found by a fishing smack and taken into Milford. Captain Lewer and six men were in the third boat and they were picked up an hour after the ship sank and landed at Milford by the *Syntra*, of Dublin. Two lifeboats left the *Sovereign* before she sank. That with Captain Putnam and eight men was seen at 7.30 on Thursday morning off the Pembrokeshire coast by Captain J. Bannister, of the SS *Bay Fisher*, of Barrow, which picked them up. They were suffering from exposure after thirty hours and landed at Port Talbot on Thursday evening and taken care of by David Jenkins, honorary agent of the Shipwrecked Mariners' Society, before leaving for Cardiff. The five men in the other boat from the *Sovereign* were not found.

The SS *Benamain*, of London, was bound from Swansea for Le Tréport (northern France) with a general cargo including fifty tons of copper ingots produced by the Swansea firm of Vivian and Sons. At 4.10 pm on 28 March 1890 she ran ashore on Lundy's east coast. The ship was got off next day and steamed back for Swansea but sank off Oxwich on the Gower coast. Her crew of twelve were picked up by the pilot cutter *Rival* and landed at Swansea.

The SS *Ashdale*, of Glasgow, was built at Grangemouth in 1883 and was a regular trader between Cardiff and Tralee, Ireland. She left Cardiff at 2 pm on 9 September 1890, her cargo and bunkers totalling 310 tons. The pilot left off Nash Point at 5.30. At 1.10 am next day, when to the west of Lundy, the chief engineer Thomas Darnell ran on deck to tell Captain James Brown that water was gushing into the engine room. All hands abandoned in the boats and saw the ship sink stern first half an hour later. They got ashore on the island and were landed at Clovelly by the Trinity House vessel *Irene* which had the Elder Brethren aboard carrying out an inspection of lighthouses. The Board of Trade inquiry heard that the vessel had probably been damaged on the last trip to Tralee having struck bottom a number of times in the canal which connects the town to the sea. The master's certificate was suspended for six months and the engineer ordered to pay a penalty of £20.

The SS *Gladiolus*, of North Shields, 1,224 tons register, Captain George Wright, left Cardiff at 9.30 on the morning of 1 March 1891 bound for St Lucia with 2,243 tons of coal. A dense fog set in and she steamed at very low speed on a course to pass south of Lundy. The lead was used constantly and a sharp look out was held for the lights and fog signals of Bull Point and Lundy. Nothing was seen or heard. The ship stranded on Lundy at 1.50 am the next day and got off on the flood tide at 6 am with her fore hold flooded. She was able to steam back to Cardiff where it was found that part of her stem had been torn off. At the Board of Trade inquiry it was heard that there was no evidence that fog rockets had been fired from Lundy and the magistrate and nautical assessors found that the master and mate were not at fault.

The SS *Fatfield*, of London, had been built in 1865 and was of 417 tons register. She traded regularly between the South Wales coal ports and France. She left the West Bute Dock, Cardiff, at 9.30 on the evening of Saturday 21 November 1891 with 850 tons of coal for Le Havre. At 6.30 the next morning she was about seven miles south-east of Lundy when the donkeyman ran up to the bridge to tell Captain Alfred Moore that water was pouring into the engine room. The pumps had been started but the water was gaining on them. The two lifeboats were launched and all twelve men abandoned ship. The boats had pulled away 200 yards when the *Fatfield* went down. As they rowed towards Lundy, the SS *Pembridge*, of London, hove to, picked them up and landed them at Cardiff that evening.

The SS *Tunisie*, of Bordeaux, 1,604 tons gross, left Cardiff with coal for Marseilles on Thursday 18 February 1892. The wind was from the north-east and soon snow was falling thickly. The ship ran ashore on the Sugar Loaf near the south end of Lundy at about 5.30 am the next day. The snow was so thick that the crew had been unable to see the vessel's bows let alone the island. Seas broke over the ship and wrecked the lifeboats, preventing the crew abandoning. At dawn they were seen by John McCarthy the principal lighthouse keeper. As there was no rocket life-saving apparatus (breeches buoy) on the island, McCarthy tried using fog signal rockets to throw a line onto the ship. A couple of shots failed but then he got a line aboard. This was then used by the crew to pull a heavier line down and McCarthy and his assistants rigged a strong coal bag to the line. Using this they drew all twenty-one members of the crew up the cliff one at a time. An island family allowed the crew to use their home until they were taken up to Cardiff on Friday 26 February by the tug *Sea Prince*. The Mount Stuart Dry Dock company began salvage and the *Tunisie* was towed to Cardiff by the tugs *Falcon* and *Sea Prince* on Wednesday 30 March. The ship proved to be too badly damaged to be worth repairing and was taken out of dock and run ashore on Penarth beach to be broken up. At their meeting in April the Royal National Lifeboat Institution voted their thanks on vellum to John McCarthy and awarded him, his two assistant keepers and eight others who had taken part in the rescue of the crew of the *Tunisie* fifteen shillings each.

The SS *Ackworth*, of West Hartlepool, 2,150 tons gross, sailed from Cardiff on the morning of 20 April 1892 bound for Port Said with 2,760 tons of coal. The vessel ran ashore in fog at Tibbetts Point on Lundy's east coast at nine that evening. The ship's bow ran up onto the rocks flooding the fore-hold and the water ran back into the engine room and aft hold. The Glasgow tug *Flying Elf* took off Captain George Kennedy and twenty-three crew and landed them at Cardiff. The salvage crew removed the cargo from the fore-hold allowing a strong wooden platform to be built over

THE "ACKWORTH" ASHORE AT LUNDY ISLAND.

the damaged hull. The vessel was got off and towed to Cardiff by the tugs *Falcon, Sea Prince, Advance* and *Salisbury* on 28 May and entered the Mount Stuart Dry Dock. The Board of Trade inquiry found that the master and second mate were to blame but returned their certificates.

On 12 November 1892 a boat landed a body at Tenby which it had found in its trawl when fishing near Lundy. It was identified as that of Hugo Turnbull Pohl, a passenger aboard the new tug *Secret* which had left Lytham, Lancashire, on 25 October bound for London. The tug, its six crew and three passengers were probably victims of the severe storm which had struck the west coast of Britain on 27 October.

The SS *Charles W. Anderson*, bound from Cardiff for St Nazaire with coal, ran ashore at Lundy in dense fog on Sunday 13 August 1893. Lloyd's signal station reported that she was lying on an even keel on the telegraph cable near the landing place. Cargo was discharged from the fore-hold and she floated at 4 pm and was able to proceed.

On Thursday 16 November 1893 the SS *Boileau* left Cardiff with coal for Bordeaux. At 4 pm she was between Bull Point and Lundy when a ketch was seen flying distress signals. The steamer approached the ketch which signalled "Our vessel is unmanageable and filling with water; will you take us on board?". It was the *Favourite*, of Bideford, which was owned by H. Dadds of Ilfracombe, and was bound for Porthcawl. Captain Robson, master of the *Boileau*, ordered the lifeboat launched and it was manned by the mate D. Martin, and seamen William Doherty, Jack Garner and Carl Lundin who rowed for the ketch. The strong wind and high seas drove them back to the steamer which attempted to tow them into a better position. The boat capsized and all four were thrown into the sea. It was now dark. Jack Garner held onto a life-line while the other three climbed onto the keel. They drifted away from the *Boileau* and after five hours Garner was seized with cramp. His mates pulled him up and the boat righted. They bailed it out and, using a line and two oars, rigged a sea-anchor which kept the boat's bow to the seas. Soon after dawn on Friday they saw a brig and tied a rag to an oar which they raised. They were spotted and picked up by the *Jeune Charles* which landed them at Swansea. The *Favourite* drifted north and when it neared Carmarthen Bay late morning of the 17th the mate, James Sergeant, left in the boat and was rescued by the lifeboat *A Daughter's Offering* from the Port Eynon station on the Gower peninsula. The schooner *Chrysolite*, of Penzance, saw the *Favourite* and took off the master H. James and the third hand and landed them at Porthcawl. The *Boileau* arrived at Mumbles roads where Martin returned aboard but Doherty, Garner and Lundin decided that they had had enough that trip and returned to Cardiff.

The brigantine *Ismyr*, of North Shields, 209 tons, was bound from Burry Port, Carmarthenshire, with 361 tons of anthracite for Woolwich Arsenal, London. A strong west wind was experienced as they sailed down channel so they put into Lundy roads and anchored there. At about 3 am on Friday 1 December 1893 the wind flew to the north-east and blew so hard that a cable parted. The other anchor dragged and the vessel struck Rat Island. Though there were tugs in the roads, the conditions were so bad that they were unable to assist. The *Ismyr*'s master, Frederick Smith, launched the boat and got five of his crew to board it. He then let out the painter (bow rope) and the five got onto the rocks of Rat Island. Huge seas sweeping the rocks swept James Ryan, of Waterford, and Robert Ballantyne, of Newcastle, off and they were drowned. The other three, Edward O'Brien, William Pride and James Raeburn, climbed higher. Captain Smith pulled the boat back to the *Ismyr* and he, the mate George Hargreaves and the boy James Shelly got aboard. Cutting the painter they attempted to get ashore but the boat struck a rock and they were thrown into the sea before getting onto a rock ledge. Smith had taken off his sea boots and oilskins before leaving the wreck. He now swam to another ledge from which he thought they could climb the cliff.

He called to the mate to let the boy, who was wearing a lifebelt, go. The surf took the lad right into Smith's arms. The mate followed and Smith grabbed him and pulled him out. The three climbed the cliff and met the other three men. It was now snowing so they huddled together until 7.30 when they were found by an officer from Lloyd's signal station. They went to the squire's house and enjoyed breakfast and a warm fire but got no clothes until later in the day a labourer very kindly gave them jackets. The mail skiff *Gannet*, Captain Dark, landed them at Appledore and they were put up at the 'Royal George' hotel by the Shipwrecked Mariners' Society before being given tickets for home.

At midday on Tuesday 14 May 1895 thick fog was beginning to lift when the coasting steamer *Catherine Sutton*, of Cork, in ballast for Newport, collided with the Faversham brigantine *Coila* which was bound for France with anthracite loaded at Burry Port. Captain E. Appleton Court, his wife, and seven crew abandoned in the boat as the *Coila* went down between Lundy and the island of Caldy off Tenby, Pembrokeshire. They were picked up and landed at Newport the next day.

The SS *Maria*, 1,580 tons, was owned by M.J. de Poorter of Rotterdam. She left Cardiff with 3,500 tons of coal for Naples and ran ashore in dense fog one hundred yards from the landing place on Lundy at 2 am on 9 September 1895. A boat from the island landed the crew. Dobson, the Cardiff manager of Mordey, Carney & Co. Ltd, superintended the salvage and the ship was floated to a better position a week later. The *Maria* was towed to Penarth and docked there on 2 October to discharge the cargo before entering dry dock for repair.

The schooner *Lanisley*, owned by Consolidated Smelting (J.B. Bolitho & Co.), had a cargo of coal from Neath for Penzance. It is believed that she sank at about 1.15 am on Wednesday 2 October 1895 between Ilfracombe and Lundy in a force ten storm. Her master, Barzillai Beckerleg (known by his friends as Captain Barlow), was found jammed between boulders at Freshwater Bay, near Lee (west of Ilfracombe), by a man who was gathering laver. It was many hours before he could be removed from the beach and he died soon after. The mate Richard Thomas, and crew John Davis, Samuel Warren, Philip Jelbart and Arthur Downing were not found. The *Clipper*, of Bridgwater, was bound from London to Bristol with Portland cement. She too was struck by the storm and her sails torn to ribbons. She drove towards Hartland and her crew abandoned in the boat which capsized. A Danish seaman drowned but the rest of the crew including Captain James Exon and the mate Robert McCormick were got ashore by Hartland coastguard. Captain Exon died of exhaustion later that day. A tug arrived and towed the *Clipper* to Lundy roads.

There had been bad weather for some days and vessels were wind bound at Swansea. Then on Thursday 19 March 1896 there was a fair wind and the bay was described as "a sea of masts" as vessels left the docks and made their way down channel. Late that evening the 88 ton schooner *Zenith*, of Falmouth, with coal for the Guernsey Steam Towing Co., was in collision eight miles from Lundy with the 130 ton schooner *Forest Belle*, of Newport, which had coal for Chatham. The wind had risen again and a near gale was blowing. The *Forest Belle* struck the *Zenith* on the port bow carrying away her bulwarks, stoving in the stem and ripping open the side. George Watson, a member of the crew, was knocked overboard and got hold of the *Forest Belle*'s bowsprit which was damaged and hanging down. He got aboard the *Forest Belle* which returned to Swansea for repair. Initially it was thought that the rest of the *Zenith*'s crew had drowned when it sank. In fact Captain Lacolley, who was a Jerseyman, the mate James Wesley of Falmouth, George Latour of Cannes and John Sullivan of Swansea had got away in the *Zenith*'s boat. They rigged a sea-anchor and this kept the boat's bow to the sea and let her drift up channel. At daylight they saw the Helwick lightship off Gower and an hour or so later they were taken on board. At 5 pm on Friday they got aboard the SS *Norseman* which towed their boat up to Penarth and landed them there.

The ketch *Kate* was loaded with materials for St Helen's church which was being built on Lundy. She dragged her anchors in heavy seas on 20 May 1896 and drove ashore on the landing beach. Captain Popham and brothers Robert and John Souch were able to get ashore. Initial reports suggested that the ketch was a total wreck but she was towed to Appledore where the badly damaged starboard side was repaired.

The Danish brigantine *Tre Søstre* left Cardiff with coal for Lisbon on the evening of 4 October 1896. At about three o'clock the next morning she was in collision in thick fog off Lundy with the Padstow schooner *Emily* which was bound for Newport in ballast. The *Emily* picked up Captain Petersen and six hands of the brigantine and stood by until the vessel sank an hour later. The Danes were landed at Newport and taken to the Elliott Home for Seamen.

Bristol Channel pilots

BEFORE the industrial revolution led to the development of ports in South Wales, Bristol was the major port on this stretch of water, and Bristol's status as England's second city in the seventeenth century resulted in its name being given to what previously had been called "The Severn Sea". However, Bristol is at the lowest bridging point of the River Avon, seven miles from the sea, and the original docks were an integral part of the city centre. Safe navigation of the tidal river, coupled with one of the largest tidal ranges in the world, made local knowledge essential. The village of Pill, on a creek which flows into the south side of the Avon halfway between Bristol and Avonmouth, was the traditional home of the pilots who guided ships to and from Bristol Docks.

Pilot skiffs at Pill c. 1910

In 1863 there were 74 licensed Bristol Pilots, with 45 named boats. They all worked from the creek at Pill, and each pilot came from a Pill family.

Pilot cutters or pilot skiffs were fast and seaworthy boats, sailed by two people (often the owner and a boy apprentice). They would carry a pilot, sometimes two, and they operated in competition with each other, racing to be the first to reach an incoming ship and get the job of piloting her safely to port. Pilot skiffs could be at sea for days in all weathers.

On the west coast of Lundy is a former landing place called Pilots Quay. There is no documentary evidence for the origin of the name, but it is a reminder of the days when pilot skiffs played an essential role in safe navigation in Lundy waters.

1896-1897: Seventeen drown and two survive when the *Rajah* sinks

THE SS *Springwell*, of Sunderland, was on passage from Liverpool to Swansea when at 5.15 on the morning of Thursday 10 December 1896 cries for help were heard when the ship was north of Lundy. In the heavy seas Captain Chisholm failed to get his ship near so ordered the mate Guy Potts to launch the lifeboat. Potts took Anderson the carpenter, McGuire the bosun, and seamen Hughes and Flynn and they pulled away. In the darkness, strong wind and high seas it took them an hour to get to a waterlogged boat in which they saw two men standing up to their waists in water and much swollen by the salt and cold. The two were Germans who spoke a little English. They were taken back to the *Springwell* and landed at Swansea that day. As soon as they were fit they went to the offices of Captain Friedrich Dahne, the German consul at Swansea, where they told their story to journalists. The men were Friedrich Wilt and Herman Loper, members of the crew of the 1,230 ton full-rigged ship *Rajah*, of Bremen, which had left Barry with a cargo of coal for Hong Kong on Tuesday 8 December. When off Lundy that evening the ship ran into a severe gale. The vessel was badly damaged, her cargo probably shifted, and by the next morning she sank. The second mate (whose name was not recorded), seamen Heinrich Holtz, Wilt and Loper got aboard a lifeboat which was badly damaged and without oars. They saw a few other members of the crew in the sea but the conditions prevented them assisting. In a short while they were alone, the boat was waterlogged and kept afloat only because it had watertight compartments at bow and stern. The next day the second mate and Holtz were so weak they were washed overboard. As soon as Wilt and Loper heard the *Springwell* approaching they found enough energy to shout for help. The master and sixteen hands of the *Rajah* had drowned.

The London tug *Red Rose* was between Bull Point and Lundy on 23 January 1897 when a pilot cutter was seen in distress in the heavy seas built up by a northerly storm. The tug took the *Mystery* No. 11, of Barry, in tow, its mast having fallen. The *Mystery*'s master, Hancock, asked to be towed to Ilfracombe but after five hours the tow parted. He and his crew of two were taken off as the cutter sank and were landed at Ilfracombe before leaving in a steamer for Cardiff.

The Brixham trawler *Diamond* was fishing off Trevose when a strong gale blew in and she made for the lee of Lundy roads. During the night of 3 March 1897 the SS *Springbok*, of Llanelli, which was anchored near, dragged her anchors at the height of the gale and struck the *Diamond* broadside-on bringing down her port rigging. The steamer's propeller then struck the trawler's stern, holing it. The *Diamond*'s crew, Hampson Buley master, John Mitchelmore mate, Sam Towell, Robert Popham and the boy William Buley, scrambled aboard the *Springbok* which had lost its propeller. The steamer was towed to Cardiff by the tug *Elliot and Jeffrey*.

Lundy was enveloped in dense fog on Saturday morning 20 March 1897. Some men working for Trinity House on the north lighthouse were rowing up the east coast near Tibbetts Point when they saw the dim outline of a vessel approaching. They shouted a warning and the ship's engines were put astern. It did run ashore but was not badly damaged. It was the SS *Cam* bound from Barry to Port Said with coal. The vessel floated as the tide made and returned to Barry with her fore compartment flooded. At about seven that evening the SS *Salado*, of London, 2,187 tons gross, 1,405 net, left Newport with 2,554 tons of coal for Buenos Aires. She had a crew of twenty-two and three passengers, two of whom were the master's sons. The fog had not lifted and the *Salado* ran ashore at the Mousehole at about 4.40 am on Sunday 21 March. The ship's fore-peak was soon flooded. Two kedge anchors were laid out from the stern but as the tide rose they failed to hold and the

Salado went broadside onto the rocks. The tug *Royal Briton* took off the first officer Alexander Burn, passenger Percy Rolfe and the master's sons and landed them at Ilfracombe. Burn telegraphed the owners and the passengers left for London by train. On the next ebb the vessel broke in two. The master and crew had got ashore and lodged in the cottages at Lloyd's signal station. The wreck was auctioned at Cardiff Exchange, the hull realising £355, the stores just £5, the cargo of Risca black vein steam coal £16-10s and the 600 tons of bunker coal just £1-5s. The salvage company, Forsdyke & Edwards, of Cardiff, may well have taken on more than they could manage as the work went on for well over a year. Two vessels working at the wreck were themselves lost. On 1 November 1897 the SS *Ballydoon*, of Glasgow, put a pump and boiler on the *Salado* but with the wind strong from the east then sought shelter on the west coast. She sank and her crew were taken aboard the tug *Victoria*, of Newport. Then on 31 August 1898 the unmanned salvage hulk *Rover* which had been taking gear and machinery from the wreck sank alongside. Captain James Rainnie, master of the *Salado*, was found responsible for the loss for steaming at too great a speed in the fog and for not having used the lead often enough. His certificate was suspended for three months.

The 50 ton ketch *Millicent*, of and for Padstow from Newport with coal, was anchored in Lundy roads sheltering from a south-west gale when the wind suddenly shifted to north-east and drove her ashore on 1 April 1897. Captain Hoskin and his crew of two got ashore but had lost all their belongings.

The ketch *Infanta*, of Padstow, was at Lundy on 19 May 1897 to load granite for Fremington. She drove ashore and was wrecked. Her master Joseph Leslie and the crew of two got ashore.

Aftermath of a shipwreck (*The Cardiff Times* 8 January 1898)

A WRECK OFF LUNDY.

ALLEGED ROBBERY FROM THE SALADO

At Devon Quarter Sessions on Wednesday Jas. Binding, diver, Cardiff, on bail, was indicted for stealing copper steam piping, value £16, from the ship Salado, wrecked at Lundy Island, the property of Morgan Edwards and another, between 1st August and 3rd September last. Mr Hawke appeared for the prosecution, and Mr Bodilly, who defended, was instructed by Mr Morgan Rees, solicitor, of Cardiff. The wreck was purchased by Morgan Edwards, Rowland, and Ford for £375. It was subsequently discovered the ship had been stripped, and the piping and other parts of the vessel were missing. Some of the missing piping, the prosecution alleged, had been disposed of by the prisoner.

James Skern, marine dealer, proved buying over a hundredweight of piping from the prisoner on the 25th September. He said he had dredged it up in the Channel. Morgan Edwards identified the piping as part of the Salado. Prisoner had admitted to him (Edwards) that he made a fine mess of it, and said the watchman, Hambly, left in charge, had given him the piping. William Rowland stated that the prisoner told him he had fetched some from the ship, given Ford some and sold the rest. He added, "For God's sake do what you can for me." Ford spoke to prisoner bringing back three pipes. The prisoner afterwards said he had kept back two and sold one. He asked witness to try to get him out of it.

Mr Bodilly, in defence, contended that two pipes returned were picked up beside the ship and the other three disposed of by the prisoner at such distance that he did not think it possible they could belong to it.

Frederick Hambly, master mariner, spoke to several lengths of copper and four iron pipes being washed overboard during heavy seas. One midnight he heard hammering going on on deck, and on shouting at the men they swore and threw a bolt at him. When the prisoner visited the ship he saw him dredge up some pipes near the ship and something which he could not distinguish some distance off. He took no pipes from the ship. A good deal of property had been taken from the ship, Ford valuing what was lost at £400.

Frank Gaston, one of the hands on the prisoner's smack, deposed to the pipe being dredged up near the vessel.

The jury found prisoner "Not guilty," and he was discharged.

Ships lost 1898 to 1905

In the early hours of 9 January 1898 the schooner *Westward*, of St Ives, which was bound from Waterford for Truro with a cargo of oats, was about 15 miles south-west of Lundy. She was struck by the SS *Mandalay*, of Whitby, which was bound from Cardiff to Smyrna (now İzmir, western Türkiye). The steamer's stem cut straight through the deck and coaming of the schooner's hatch so the *Westward* sank rapidly. Captain Tindle of the *Mandalay* acted promptly and picked up the schooner's crew, Captain William Nicholas, Henry Adams the mate and seamen Walter Payne and Fred Cougar, and landed them at St Ives.

Friday 25 March 1898 saw a severe gale blow from the north which caused many wrecks over Britain. The schooner *Catherine Hendry*, of Aberystwyth, was bound from Cardiff to Ballyhack, County Wexford, with coal. At ten that morning she was to the south of St Govans on the Pembrokeshire coast when she was driven south towards Lundy. Huge seas were breaking over her deck and she was slowly sinking. The distress signal she flew was seen by the Brixham trawler *Fear Not* which stood by. The crew of the schooner, Captain Evan Jones, William K. Roberts the mate, seaman David Jones and the boy Owen K. Roberts, launched their boat and had quite a battle with the huge seas before getting to the trawler. As soon as they got aboard their boat sank. They were landed at Milford the next day into the care of the Shipwrecked Mariners' Society and given rail tickets to get home to Porthmadog.

The *Guiding Star* had been found off Lundy with both masts gone and her hull seriously damaged. There was no sign of the crew. She was towed to Milford by the Brixham smacks *Jessie* and *Prudential* on 1 May 1898. Then the Norwegian barque *P.C. Petersen* arrived at Bristol to unload her cargo of resin and turpentine from Brunswick, Georgia, and reported that she had run down the *Guiding Star* while it was trawling and had picked up the skipper Frank Humphrey, the mate Bill Cronin and two lads.

The SS *Port Darwin* bound from Cardiff to Venice ran ashore on Lundy on 16 October 1898. She got off and returned to Cardiff with her fore-hold flooded.

The paddle-tug *Earl of Jersey*, owned by Martin & Marquand, of Cardiff, was at Lundy on the lookout for inward bound ships. On Monday 28 November 1898 the wind, blowing from north-east, was at near gale force. The tug was on the west side of the island and struck a sunken rock at about 10.50 am. She began to sink so the crew left in the boat and rowed to the tug *Royal Briton* which was just a mile off. Captain William Albert and his crew of Pruett, Lovell, Samuel, Williams and Rayer were landed at Ilfracombe that evening and taken care of by the Shipwrecked Mariners' Society. The *Earl of Jersey* was well known in the Bristol Channel as she had worked as a pleasure steamer in the summer months.

A storm from the south-west struck on 7 April 1899. The Ramsgate trawler *Spitfire* capsized at 5 am that day off Lundy. She righted but had lost her mast and the boat and all gear on deck was swept away. The hull was flooded so the crew anchored and used buckets to bail her as the pump was choked. That afternoon William Vanhear was kneeling at the hatch lifting a bucket when a huge sea struck and swept him overboard where he drowned. The outward-bound steamer *D. Roma*, of Hamburg, bore down an hour later but was unable to launch its boat due to the tremendous seas. Lines were thrown to the crew who fastened them round their waists and they jumped overboard and were dragged aboard. The *Spitfire*'s skipper and owner, S. Blackman, and three crew Sisley, Doughty and Warman were given clean clothes by the Germans and enjoyed coffee and food. Later the steamer met the *Gannet* returning from Lundy which took them aboard and landed them at Appledore. There the Shipwrecked Mariners' Society looked after them and assisted them to return to Ramsgate.

The ketch-rigged smacks *Escort*, of Milford, and *Fish Girl*, of Brixham, left Milford between 2 and 3 pm on 20 April 1899 for the fishing grounds eighteen miles to the west of Lundy. They sailed in company for a few hours but then the *Escort* pulled ahead and arrived at the grounds at about 2.30 on the morning of the 21st. Her crew of four were all on deck taking in the sails to lie-to until daylight. Shortly before 3 o'clock a starboard light was seen under the port rigging and in two minutes the *Escort* was struck at right angles on its port side by the *Fish Girl*. The *Escort* was holed and sank immediately. John Pine, the skipper, and his son James, the third hand, got aboard the *Fish Girl* which launched its boat but Jasper Parnell the second hand and James Acott the boy had drowned. The *Fish Girl* remained in the area for two hours and got back to Milford by mid-day. The Board of Trade inquiry was held at the Market Hall, Brixham, on 9-10 May. It heard that it was standard practice on Brixham trawlers to have just one man on deck when not fishing – this was contrary to the rules. Seaward Sydenham, the *Fish Girl*'s second hand, was alone on deck and then went below to tell the skipper, John Brusey, that they had arrived at the fishing ground. As he returned to the deck he saw they were heading for the *Escort* but as he reached the wheel they collided. The inquiry found both the skipper and second hand to be in default. Brusey's certificate was suspended for three months and Sydenham's for six.

The SS *Kaisow*, of London, 3,921 tons gross, was owned by the China Mutual Navigation Company. She was bound from Newport to Chinese ports with a general cargo when she ran ashore in thick fog near the beach at the southern end of Lundy on 22 May 1899. The tug *Lady Lewis*, which was in the roads, was unable to get her off, but later that day the ship did float at high tide. The *Lady Lewis* was joined by the tugs *Clarissa* and *Eagle* in towing the *Kaisow* to Barry for discharge and repair. The Admiralty court ordered the following salvage awards – *Lady Lewis* £1,800 and £1,650 each to the *Clarissa* and *Eagle*.

The schooner *Star*, of St Ives, was bound for St Agnes with a cargo of coal from Port Talbot when she struck the Needle rock on Lundy's west coast in calm but very foggy conditions on Thursday 6 July 1899. Captain Lloyd and two crew abandoned in the boat as the vessel broke up. On Friday evening they were landed at Appledore by Captain Dark.

The barque *Ohr*, of Christiansand (Norway), left Cardiff with coal for Maranham, Brazil, on 10 September 1899. She was towed to Nash Point and then made sail. Soon after midnight she was approaching the north of Lundy when struck on the port quarter by the London steamer *Drayton* which cut right through the hull and she sank in just three minutes. All twelve members of the crew were thrown in the sea. Two swam to the cabin roof and climbed aboard while three others took hold of the carpenter's bench. Captain French of the *Drayton* had two lifeboats launched and these picked up Captain Edwardsen and eight men. The *Drayton* continued to search until after dawn but found no one else. The *Ohr*'s carpenter, steward and a seaman had drowned. The *Drayton*, which was bound from Garston to Barry, landed the survivors and entered the graving dock with part of the barque's mizzen mast through the plates of her port bow.

The SS *Bath City*, 2,431 tons, was owned by Charles Hill & Sons of Bristol. She was bound home from New York with a general cargo which included machinery for Bristol tramways. She passed the Fastnet light on the Irish coast and set course to pass north of Lundy. The sea was rough and there was fog though it was not thick. At about 10 pm on 23 February 1900 a light was seen to the south-east. Captain Richard Jones identified it as the light on Hartland Point and estimated he was just two miles off. The course was changed to north-west by west to pass west of Lundy in order to take a fresh departure from Lundy's north light. At about 11.15 Lundy's south light was seen on the starboard beam and full speed astern was ordered but before the way was taken off the ship struck the rocks. The report of the Board of Trade inquiry states that the ship struck on the south-west end of the island. However initial reports stated that the ship struck the Needle rock. The ship was backed off and the lifeboats launched. Fourteen men had boarded but the painters were then let go to allow the boats to get away from the ship as heavy seas were damaging them against the hull. The rest of the crew slid down the falls into the sea to get aboard but Thomas Petherick was drowned. The *Bath City* sank in deep water within twenty minutes. One lifeboat got to the roads and its men with Captain Jones were picked up by the tug *Flying Serpent*. The SS *Kingsley* picked up thirteen men from the other boat and returned to Swansea to land them. When the owners heard of the wreck they sent the tug *Sea Prince* down to the island to bring Captain Jones and the rest of the crew to Bristol. The Board of Trade inquiry concluded that the ship had not been navigated with proper and seamanlike care by Captain Jones but in view of his long and successful career it suspended his certificate for just three months.

The 23 ton fishing vessel *Skart* (the name given to cormorants in the Hebrides), of Milford, had been bought at auction in May 1902. On 26 August that year she had five tons of fish and was returning from the grounds off the north-west of Lundy when a serious leak developed. Her distress signals were seen by the steamer *Plover*, of Portreath, which took her in tow. The hawser parted in the heavy swell and the *Skart* foundered shortly after her crew had got aboard the *Plover* which landed them at Hayle that evening.

The ketch *Fiona*, 53 tons, was bound home for Jersey with coal from Newport when she sheltered in Lundy roads from a south-west gale on the evening of Friday 6 May 1904. The wind dropped soon after midnight as it veered to the north-east but as the anchor was weighed the ketch drifted onto the rocks below the Quarter Wall. Captain Warren and three crew abandoned and got ashore. At 8.20 that morning Lloyd's received the following message: "Ketch *Fiona* on rocks on east side. Crew safe. Tug *Hercules* with her rope fast trying to tow off. Think will have little or no damage. Wind NNE fresh breeze, clear, fine. Heavy ground sea". Then at 9.10 this message was sent: "*Fiona* holed in bottom seriously. Tug failed to move her. Deck awash. Crew attempted to save clothes and gear. At 9.00 she capsized on starboard side and is now submerged". The *Hercules* picked up the crew and landed them at Falmouth on Sunday.

The SS *Tyne*, of Newcastle, Captain H. Wright, was bound from St Malo for Swansea when a boat was seen at seven o'clock on the morning of 11 July 1904 fourteen miles to the south of Lundy. The *Tyne* hove to and picked up skipper Thomas Rowlands, two engineers, two trimmers, two fishermen and the boy of the Grimsby trawler *Hungate* which had foundered to the west of Lundy ten hours earlier. The *Hungate*, formerly named *Florence*, had left Milford for the fishing grounds off Portugal but developed a serious leak in a gale and her crew were forced to take to the boat on the evening of the 10th, just minutes before the trawler sank. They were hoping to reach the coast near Hartland when picked up. The men were landed at the Prince of Wales dock at Swansea and taken to the Sailor's Home and then left for Milford having been given rail tickets by the Shipwrecked Mariners' Society.

At 11.30 on the evening of Thursday 22 March 1906 the schooner *C.S. Atkinson*, of Chester, was in collision to the east of Lundy with the SS *Giuseppina Ilardi*, of Genoa. The schooner, which had been bound from Portsmouth for Swansea with scrap metal, sank within three minutes. Her mate, Benjamin Hughes, got aboard the steamer along the foreyard. Captain Humphrey Bennett was flung into the sea and was able to grasp a mattress which floated up. The steamer, which was bound from London for Swansea to load coal for Leghorn (Livorno, Italy), launched a boat and picked up Captain Bennett. It then spent some time searching for the other members of the crew but was not successful. Bennett and Hughes were landed at Swansea when the steamer arrived at the Prince of Wales dock on Friday. Those who drowned were able-seaman Edward Warren of London, John McDermot of Kinsale and the boy Albert Arnold aged fifteen of Guernsey.

1906: HMS *Montagu* runs ashore

HMS Montagu

Lloyd's List of Wednesday 30 May 1906 carried the following: "*Montagu* (HMS) – Lundy Island May 30 6.45 a.m. H.M. Battleship *Montagu* badly ashore at Shutter Point, full details not yet obtained. Continuous dense fog, calm, sea smooth.

"11.40 a.m. Vessel struck at 2.10 a.m. Damage as far as at present able to obtain, lost both propellers, wireless telegraphy apparatus at masthead shaken out, plates holed in bottom, mostly under fore part of starboard side. Several compartments full of water; engine-rooms, boiler-rooms and stokeholds flooded. Vessel now lying listed over heavily to starboard with water above torpedo nets, and still making more water. Assistance of government tugs coming from Queenstown, Pembroke Dock, Barry and Devonport, also other vessels. Continuous thick fog. WSW gentle breeze. Moderate ground swell.

"1.15 p.m. Bottom pierced by rocks in several places. Ship alive fore and aft, but on ebb tide and towards low water expect her position will be much more dangerous. Crew all saved and standing by ship. Continuous dense fog back of island, now clear off roadstead."

The *Montagu* was taking part in wireless trials when the fog, which has claimed so many victims on Lundy, gained its largest prize. No lives were lost. It was soon realised that the vessel could not be refloated so her guns were salvaged and the wreck of the hull sold for less than £5,000. The remains were scrapped over many years. Campbell's White Funnel paddle steamers ran trips from Ilfracombe for passengers to view the wreck.

Very many postcards were produced which show the *Montagu* in various stages of salvage/dilapidation.

HMS *Montagu* on the rocks (A Valentine postcard). This is not long after the accident; she appears intact and the flags are flying

Postcard published by S.J. Allen of Pembroke Dock. Salvage attempts are well under way

Construction of a ropeway to the wreck (Postcard by Twiss Brothers, Ilfracombe)

Salvaging the *Montagu*'s guns (A Twiss Brothers photo)

HMS *Montagu* – A tale of two shells …

Derek Green, now Lundy's General Manager, remembers an adventure from the days when the world was different …

It was 1991 when we were staying on Lundy for our annual week's diving with Appledore sub-Aqua club, staying in the Quarters and diving from the Appledore shipyard tug the *Lundy Puffin*.

At the time the island wanted to open a museum and had the idea to place two shells from HMS *Montagu* on either side of the doorway of the building. Having dived the wreck of the *Montagu* for many years, we were familiar with the scattering of ordnance across the seabed, so, following a request from the island, we began to plan the retrieval of two 12-inch shells.

After a recce dive to identify the two shells in question, they were subsequently raised using lifting bags and lashed unceremoniously onto the stern of the *Puffin (left)*.

This was in the days before risk assessment had been invented, but we were acutely aware that the shells were live and even though they had been underwater for around 80 years, we treated them with a bit of caution. The *Puffin* was a steel vessel, so she steamed carefully back to the landing bay, avoiding any sudden jarring of the boat.

On reaching the Landing Bay, we waited until high water and brought the boat in as close to shore as we could, and carefully lowered the shells into the shallows. When the tide went out, the island's JCB came down and scooped them both up in its front bucket and bounced them all the way up to the workshop.

Given that they were still live, the island arranged for two chaps to come from Plymouth to de-fuse them to make them safe by removing the firing mechanism and cordite. However, after a couple of days of wrenching, hammering and banging the first shell, they gave up and it looked like we would have to return them to the wreck. After day three, we were discussing the problem in the Marisco Tavern, when an old chap suggested that the firing mechanism might be left-hand threaded …

The next day they tackled the second shell and easily removed the fuse and cordite, but the first shell was so badly damaged that it had to be taken back down to the beach. It was dropped in at low water, but bad weather prevented its subsequent retrieval, and it still lies there today, occasionally visible on big spring tides. The island gave up the idea and the other shell sits outside the Blacksmith's shed *(right)* as a reminder of one of the Royal Navy's most expensive errors.

Lundy's designated wrecks

HMS *Montagu* is one of four wrecks around Lundy to have statutory designation. Historic wrecks are either "protected" under the Protection of Wrecks Act 1973 or "scheduled" under the Ancient Monuments and Archaeological Areas Act 1979. "Protected" means that a licence is needed to dive on them, either as part of a team or on a diver trail. A scheduled site can be visited by divers but is protected from interference, such as the removal of objects.

HMS *Montagu* herself is a Scheduled Monument. The scheduling was designated on 17 September 2019, following archaeological investigation by Wessex Archaeology working with Operation Nightingale, a military initiative developed to use archaeology as a means of aiding the recovery of service personnel injured in recent conflict.

The other scheduled wreck is the *South Australian* (p.51), designated on 8 November 2019.

The other two wrecks are "protected". The Gull Rock wreck isn't mentioned in this book because there are no written records of it or its sinking. It is believed to be that of a fifteenth- to sixteenth-century vessel and is represented only by cannon and stone cannon balls. A Genoese carrack is recorded as being wrecked on Lundy in 1418. The wreck was designated on 12 February 1990.

The *Iona*, in this context more usually referred to as the *Iona II* (p.26), was designated on 6 December 1989, again following work by the Archaeological Diving Unit of Wessex Archaeology. This wreck lies within the Lundy Marine Nature Reserve. A number of individuals hold visitor licences for *Iona II*.

The *Iona* is the most complete wreck of these four – though not as complete as that of the *Robert* (p.77) which lies nearby – and is important for the study of marine construction techniques of the period and especially the unique features of this vessel which was an advanced example of its type. Like all wrecks, it has also become a home for many types of marine life, both those who literally live on the wreck – anemones of various species, cup corals – and those, such as fish, lobster and conger eels, for whom it is a shelter and a hunting ground.

A Dive Trail has been published for the *Iona II* which is available in the Lundy shop. It is for a more general readership than just divers intending to visit the site and contains sections on the construction of the ship and what remains to be seen underwater; the history of the ship and its context in Glasgow shipbuilding; the rich marine life on the wreck; and information about the surveys and archaeology of the *Iona* and how the protection and monitoring works.

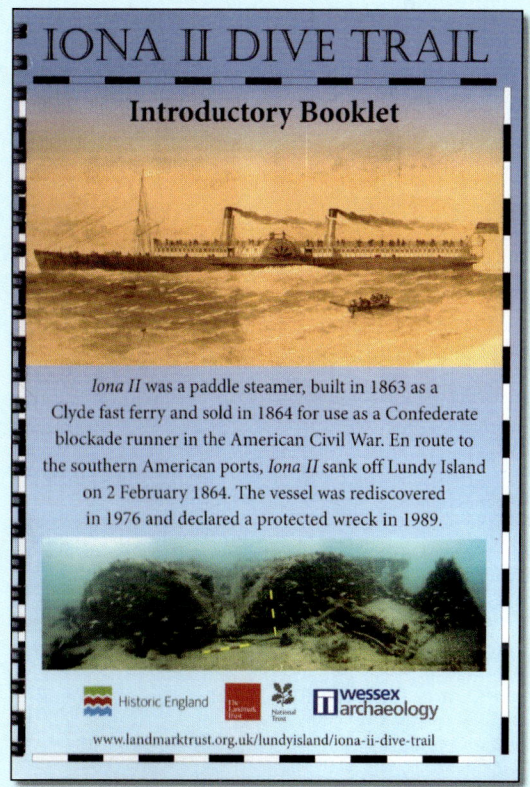

IONA II DIVE TRAIL
Introductory Booklet

Iona II was a paddle steamer, built in 1863 as a Clyde fast ferry and sold in 1864 for use as a Confederate blockade runner in the American Civil War. En route to the southern American ports, *Iona II* sank off Lundy Island on 2 February 1864. The vessel was rediscovered in 1976 and declared a protected wreck in 1989.

Historic England · The Landmark Trust · National Trust · wessex archaeology

www.landmarktrust.org.uk/lundyisland/iona-ii-dive-trail

1906-1914: Fog continues to be a menace

THE SS *Cereda*, of Bristol, 1,603 tons, outward bound from Cardiff, ran ashore in very thick fog under Lundy's granite quarries at 3 am on 22 July 1906. She floated on the rising tide two hours later and, though down by the bows, was able to steam up to Barry. She later entered Roath Dock, Cardiff, for repair.

The very next day the SS *Haxby*, bound for Newport from New York, was in collision with the schooner *Harvest Queen*, of Runcorn, about nine miles off Lundy. There was no serious damage to either vessel.

The Brixham ketch *J.E.S.S.* was fishing ten miles south-south-west of Lundy. At 8 am on 28 June 1907 the crew were hauling in the net when flames were seen coming up the companion way. In just ten minutes the vessel was a "roaring furnace" below. The crew took to the boat and were picked up by the trawler *Winnie* which landed them at Milford.

Some writers have the schooner *Dovey Belle* listed as being lost near Lundy but she actually went down forty-five miles south-south-west of Grassholm off the Pembrokeshire coast, well to the west of Lundy. The vessel was sailing from Aberdovey for Ramsgate with a cargo of slates when she was found to be leaking on the morning of Wednesday 17 July 1907. Within a couple of hours there were six feet of water in the hold. The SS *Foy* bound for Weston Point, Runcorn, arrived and began to tow her but after a few hours the tow parted and, with the schooner developing a list to starboard and the deck awash, the crew abandoned and got aboard the steamer. They were landed at Holyhead the next day. Captain John Williams and his crew got home to Aberdovey on the 20th.

In the early hours of 8 September 1907 the schooner *Spitfire* was four miles south of Lundy. There was a very thick fog and ship's sirens were heard from all quarters. The *Spitfire*, which was bound from Loctudy, Brittany, to Bristol with potatoes, was in collision with the SS *Sandhurst* which was outward bound. With her bows holed, the schooner was soon sinking. Her crew abandoned and rowed to the steamer before being transferred to a tug which landed them at Swansea.

The SS *Auricula*, of London, left Swansea with 1,055 tons of anthracite at 6 am on 1 May 1908. The master set a course which should have taken the vessel to the south of Lundy but at 10.30 land was seen and the ship struck Rat Island. Four hundred tons of cargo were discharged and the ship was floated to the landing beach. The damage to the port bow was repaired and the vessel returned to Swansea. The Board of Trade inquiry found both the master and chief officer in default and suspended their certificates for three months.

The schooner *James & Agnes*, of Lancaster, 95 tons net, had been built at Barrow in 1864 by William Ashburner, but by 1909 was owned at Arklow. The vessel loaded 220 tons of anthracite at the South Dock, Swansea, and sailed on 19 October 1909 bound for Medina Mills, near Cowes. She sailed down channel in company with the schooner *Venedocian* whose master reported that he last saw her to the east of Lundy, at nine that evening, but did not see her to the west of the island. The vessel did not arrive at the Isle of Wight and was posted missing by Lloyd's. The Board of Trade inquiry, which was held at Swansea in February 1910, concluded that she was "probably lost in collision with an unknown vessel in the vicinity of Lundy". Captain James Horan, mate Patrick Chatham, A.B. Thomas Burn, O.S. Paul Burn and the cook Michael Burn were lost.

The SS *Thistlemor*, of Sunderland, loaded 4,575 tons of coal at Cardiff and was bound for Cape Town. She left at 9 am on 2 December 1909, pilot Richards leaving when they were off the Breaksea lightship. As the ship steamed down channel the weather got steadily worse and by the evening she was battling against a full south-west storm. Heavy seas broke over the forecastle which was flooded. Then just after midnight, seas tore a ventilator from the fore well-deck and water entered the number one hold. Efforts made by the crew to plug the hole failed. The ship was then put about hoping to reach shelter in Lundy roads. The vessel was now well down by the bows and increasingly difficult to steer. Distress signals were fired from about 2.30 am on the 3rd. The SS *Arndale*, which had also been damaged by the gale, was putting back after her mate had been injured. This ship saw the *Thistlemor*'s signals and saved nine men from the lifeboat which capsized in leaving the sinking ship. The *Thistlemor* had now sunk in Barnstaple Bay with the loss of her master James Anderson and twenty-two men. The Board of Trade inquiry found that the ventilators, which were essential when carrying coal, were not sufficiently strong. There was also much criticism of the coastguard lookouts who had seen some of the ship's distress signals but had not informed Clovelly lifeboat promptly.

George Bennett, a Barry pilot, had boarded the Dutch steamer *Tromp* west of Lundy on Saturday 16 July 1910. His cutter *Linda Grace* was towed astern. The *Tromp* then altered course to avoid colliding with a schooner and its propeller struck the cutter's bow and sank it. Bennett's son John and the assistant were rescued by the steamer's punt. The 40 ft *Linda Grace* was well known as she had often won the annual Bristol Channel pilot cutter race.

On the afternoon of 16 December 1910, the trawler *Friendship*, of Brixham, was off Lundy when heavy seas struck the vessel and swept the master Richard Foster and mate Charles Stokes overboard. As they were both in heavy gear they were drowned. Hugh Keating and Fred Cheadle, who were in their teens, were now doing their best to sail the vessel which was slowly sinking. At three the next morning they were rescued by Albert Gempton and John Tidmarsh, of the trawler *Gratitude*, who were each awarded the Board of Trade silver medal and received at Buckingham Palace on 2 May 1911.

On 14 April 1911 the SS *Arosa*, of and for Villagarcia, Spain, with coal from Cardiff, collided with the SS *Racine*, of Nantes, bound from Le Havre for Swansea in ballast. The collision occurred two miles off Lundy. The *Racine* was holed and sank within twenty minutes. Captain Gerard and the crew of twenty, having left in the lifeboats, were picked up by the *Arosa* and landed at Barry where she put in for repairs to her bows.

During a strong gale in the early hours of 30 November 1912 flares were seen about six miles south-east of Lundy. The Clovelly and Ilfracombe lifeboats were launched but found that the SS *Augoustis*, of Andros, Greece, had broken down and was being towed up channel.

The SS *Breiz Huel*, 3,047 tons, Captain Andeain, left Barry with a cargo of coal on Saturday 8 March 1913 bound for Algiers. In the early hours of the next day she was in collision between Lundy and Hartland Point with the SS *Tempus*, of Cardiff, which was inward bound from Barcelona. The crew and two women passengers of the *Breiz Huel* abandoned ship. Seven of them were picked up by the SS *Orne*, Captain Jean Pierre, and landed at Barry. The remaining thirty-two got aboard the *Tempus* which stood by until the *Breiz Huel* sank twelve hours later.

On 10 December 1913 the boat of the *Mary Ashburner*, 106 tons gross, was found four miles east of Lundy. This schooner had been bound from Charlestown for Runcorn with china clay when run down in St George's Channel on 27 November by the SS *Castillian*, 1,922 tons gross, which was bound from Liverpool to Tangiers. The schooner's crew, who were drowned, were John Hughes master, William Hughes mate, a boy who was the mate's brother and two seamen whose names were not recorded. They were all from Amlwch, Anglesey.

On 28 December 1913 the pilot cutter *Emma* was waiting off Lundy for Elders and Fyffes' SS *Bayano*, which was bound from Costa Rica with passengers, mail and bananas. Pilot Edward Rowland boarded the *Bayano* but the heavy weather carried away the cutter's boom and it drifted under the ship's stern and sank after striking the propeller. Skipper Tom Stenner and his son Fred were taken aboard and landed at Avonmouth.

On 18 February 1914 the Barry cutter *Molly* put the pilot aboard the SS *Tintern Abbey* and was being towed up channel when it capsized in a heavy squall and sank off Lundy. Crew members Protheroe and Davies were picked up by the steamer's boat.

Rocket life saving apparatus

THE LOSS of ships' crews when a vessel had been driven onto the coast and a lifeboat couldn't get near was identified as a problem in the early nineteenth century. One early way to get a line from shore to ship, or vice versa, was to attach it to a mortar. The sudden acceleration involved risked breaking the line, and Henry Trengrouse is credited with inventing a rocket-propelled apparatus in 1807. In the UK, the Board of Trade became responsible for establishing and maintaining rocket life saving apparatus around the coast and for training crews. On Lundy, a substantial shed *(right)* was built in the Village (now the Museum, opposite the Shop) to house a cart and the equipment. Regular practices were held when the rocket and its line would be fired at a pole representing the mast of a ship. "Rocket poles" were once a common sight around the coast, and some remain, including the one on Lundy, which has given its name to the adjacent Rocket Pole Pond.

Martin Coles Harman, who bought Lundy in 1925, resented having "outside" authorities operating on his island and agreed with the Board of Trade in 1928 to take over the ownership and operation of the rocket life saving apparatus, which was manned by volunteer islanders. Their most notable service was to the *Taxiarchis* (p.73), when the crew were on for 24 hours without a break and then at intervals for a further 48 hours, eventually successfully landing by breeches buoy the entire ship's crew of 24 men (and the ship's cat).

The Rocket Pole and part of Rocket Pole Pond

1915-1917: Seamen face another foe

THE SS *Sambo*, of Newport, bound from Swansea to Morlaix (Brittany) with coal, sank three miles south-east of Lundy on 26 March 1915. Her crew were able to get ashore. Houlder Brothers steamer *Clutha River* 3,144 tons left Barry on 1 May 1915 with 5,268 tons of steam coal for the River Plate. In dense fog she ran ashore on Lundy and struck Gull Rock near Tibbets Point. She was towed up channel by the tug *Margaret Hain* and beached off Cardiff. With part of the cargo discharged she was taken into dock to be repaired. The cargo was offered for sale by tender.

The steamer *Cottingham*, of Glasgow, was bound in ballast from Rouen for Swansea. At 4 pm on Sunday 26 December 1915 she was sixteen miles to the south-west of Lundy when a shell passed over the ship with no warning. The conning tower of a submarine was seen about a mile astern in the ship's wake. A second shell was fired and the submarine came up on the ship's starboard quarter. The U-boat signalled "abandon ship" and fired a shell which struck the *Cottingham*'s starboard bow. Captain Colin Mitchell and five men abandoned in one boat and the chief officer and six in the other. The submarine continued firing to sink the ship. It was now getting dark and by 6 pm the two boats lost touch with one another. The master was steering north-east hoping to reach Lundy when the patrol boat *Soar* found them at 10 pm. The *Soar* searched for the other boat but failed to find it. Days later the second boat was found on the rocks at Porthllisky, Pembrokeshire. The chief officer and six men had drowned. They were Alexander McPhail, George Pearson, Lawrence Benoke, Fred Cook, Neil Grant, John Lewis of Orange Street, Swansea, and Richard Roberts also of Swansea. The submarine was the *U-24*, Rudolf Schneider commander. (On 2 July 1915 the *Cottingham* had struck *UC-2* off Great Yarmouth. Captain Mitchell reported the incident and patrol boats sank the submarine which was a minelayer.)

The ketch *Emblem*, of Bideford, was bound from Courtmacsherry, County Cork, for Bristol with a cargo of oats when she was abandoned in a sinking condition about thirty miles north-west of Lundy on 7 January 1916. Captain John Stoneman and his two crew were picked up by the Lowestoft trawler *Godrevy*, Lockwood skipper, and landed at Padstow.

On 24 July 1916 the SS *Balvenie*, 872 tons, was bound from Glasgow to St Nazaire with a cargo of railway locomotives when she collided, a few miles south-west of Lundy, in thick fog with the SS *Tagona* which was bound from Dunkirk to Swansea. Two members of the *Balvenie*'s crew, the Greek cook and seaman Murdoch McNeil, were drowned when the ship sank but the other twelve were picked up by the *Tagona* and landed at Swansea.

The schooner *Mary Orr*, 75 tons, was registered at Glasgow, though her master, Captain Gill, and crew were from Port Isaac. She was bound, in ballast, from Waterford to Appledore and sheltered in Lundy roads from a strong west gale on Sunday 17 September 1916. Shortly before 2 pm on Tuesday the Ilfracombe lifeboat launched and sailed out to Lundy and brought ashore Captain Gill and his three crew. They had abandoned the schooner on advice from a patrol boat whose crew thought that the gale would veer to the north-east and drive her ashore. The next day Captain Gill went out on the *Devonia* which towed the *Mary Orr* to Appledore.

The schooner *Edward Arthur*, of Caernarfon, 151 tons, was bound from Waterford for Bristol with a cargo of oats when she drove ashore just north of Jenny's Cove in the early hours of 2 January 1917. The mainmast fell against the cliff allowing the master and two of the crew to get ashore but the fourth man, said to be an Australian, was drowned.

On 24 June 1917 the SS *Hilversum*, of Amsterdam, 1,505 tons, was bound from Le Havre for Barry in ballast when torpedoed 5 miles west-south-west of Lundy by *UC-51*, Hans Galster commander. All the crew survived but how they got ashore seems not to have been recorded.

The SS *Knatten*, of Molde, Norway, 530 tons, was a regular trader between the South Wales ports and France. On 20 August 1917 she was bound from Swansea to St Malo with coal when she caught fire. Captain Oien and his crew did their best to fight the flames but were eventually forced to abandon ship. The vessel drifted towards Lundy, struck the Hen and Chickens rocks, and sank.

On 24 August 1917 the SS *Mount Park*, of Greenock, 1,376 tons, was bound from Newport to Dover with coal when she was in collision about six miles north-east of Lundy with the Greek ship *Alexandria*. As the crew of the *Mount Park* were about to abandon ship, the Japanese steward, Kushiro Shinoyama, came on deck with a large bowl of eggs and a plate of scones which he passed round saying "You need plenty strength in water. Here plenty eggs and scones. Eat!". Presumably one of the lifeboats sank as many of the crew of twenty spent hours in the sea. Captain Mason took hold of the second mate Lionel Robinson who became exhausted saying "Let me go I cannot keep afloat any longer". Mason did his best to hold him but Robinson drowned. A few days later four bodies were washed ashore on the Glamorgan coast – one on Kenfig beach, another at Sker Point, a third at Rest Bay, Porthcawl, and the fourth at Nash Point. The body at Rest Bay was found to have a letter in a pocket addressed to K. Shinoyama, SS *Mount Park*, Alexandra Dock, Newport. Captain Mason identified the body found at Nash Point as being Lionel Robinson. Fifteen of the crew survived and presumably were picked up by the *Alexandria*.

The schooner *Agricola*, of Cardiff, left Garston, Liverpool, with coal for Cherbourg on 5 September 1917 and at 5.30 pm on 12 September she was stopped by *U-19*, Johannes Spiess commander, about fifteen miles west-north-west of Lundy. Captain Lewis and his crew abandoned as the U-boat shelled the vessel. A scuttling charge was thrown on board and the vessel sank. The crew got to Lundy.

The *U-96*, Heinrich Jess commander, sank two fishing vessels twelve miles north of Lundy on 4 October 1917. The first was the *Rupee* BM 294, owned by William Barnard of Padstow, which went down drowning her crew of four. Then the *Young Clifford* LT 498 was sunk. Her crew survived but how they got ashore was not recorded.

The schooner *Robert Brown*, of Chester, 119 tons, was bound from Fowey for Runcorn with china clay when stopped fifteen miles north-west of Lundy by *UC-77*, Reinhard von Rabenau commander, on 19 November 1917. The schooner was sunk by a scuttling charge placed on board after Captain Hewitt and his crew had abandoned.

Then on 26 November the coal cargo of the SS *Gurley*, of Bergen, 542 tons, shifted in a strong gale and the vessel, which was bound from Swansea for Rouen, capsized a few miles to the south-west of Lundy. A motor launch went to the assistance of the crew and found Captain Iversen and the mate on a raft. They were picked up and landed at Ilfracombe. The other twelve members of the crew had abandoned in the boat and got ashore.

Just four days later the Brixham trawlers *Courage* and *Gazelle* were attacked and sunk six miles west by north of the north end of Lundy by *U-57* commanded by Carl-Siegfried von Georg. The crews got away in the boats.

1918-1939: U-boats sink hospital ships

THE hospital ship *Rewa*, 7,308 tons, was bound from Salonica to Avonmouth with 279 wounded servicemen, 80 medical staff and a crew of 207. The ship carried the green line round its hull and the huge red cross each side and was well lit. There would be no doubt that she was a hospital ship. At about 11 pm on 4 January 1918 she was to the south-west of the southern end of Lundy when the master and third officer, who were on the bridge, saw two small white lights about a mile ahead on the ship's port bow. They thought that they were shown by a sailing vessel so the course was changed to avoid it. At 11.15 the ship was struck on the port side abreast the funnel by a torpedo. Two of the lifeboats on that side were blown to pieces but fourteen boats were launched and all aboard, except for four Indian sailors who were killed by the explosion, were evacuated. The *Rewa* sank soon after midnight. The *Rewa*'s radio distress message had been received by the Aberdeen trawler *Ben Strome* which was steaming up channel in company with the oil tanker *Paul Paix*. The *Ben Strome* arrived followed by the trawler *Lark* and the tanker. The lifeboats had remained together and the trawlers and the tanker took everyone aboard. The vessels made for Swansea where a huge effort was made to assist the wounded, staff and seamen. As many had been in their night clothes and had lost all their kit, the shops of the town, including Ben Evans store, went into action. Meals were provided at Exchange Buildings, near the South Dock, and the YMCA. R.E. Jones' café and Hotel Metropole also played a part in looking after everyone. The torpedo had been fired by *U-55*, Wilhelm Werner commander. Germany denied that they had sunk the ship and claimed that it had probably struck a British mine. Captain George Legge, master of the tanker *Paul Paix*, lived at St Thomas, Swansea, and was given a gold watch by the *Rewa*'s owners, British-India Steam Navigation Company, who sent £25 to be divided amongst his crew.

On 14 February 1918 the schooner *Bessie Stephens*, of and from Fowey, was bound for Preston with china clay when stopped by *U-86*, Helmut Patzig commander, ten miles west of Lundy. The schooner was sunk by the U-boat. The crew of five were picked up next day by the SS *Carnalea* which landed them at Penzance. (In June that year the *U-86* would sink the hospital ship *Llandovery Castle* off the Irish coast. Under Patzig's orders the U-boat rammed the ship's lifeboats and opened fire on survivors including nurses in the sea. There were just twenty-four survivors out of the 258 people aboard. After the war Patzig returned to his native Danzig and was able to avoid trial at Leipzig.)

The hospital ship *Glenart Castle*, 6,824 tons, was bound from Newport for Brest. The commander of a naval vessel reported that at 1.30 am on 25 February 1918 he was 10 miles south-south-east of the Scarweather lightship when he sighted the *Glenart Castle*. The weather was fine and with bright moonlight, the green band around the vessel together with the red cross on the port side were easily visible from his position four miles south of the ship. The ship appeared to be heading towards the north end of Lundy. A member of the crew of the *Glenart Castle*, who lived at Newport, described what happened at 4 am when the ship was twenty miles west of the island. "There was an explosion. I was in my bunk and went on deck in pyjamas. Most of the boats on the starboard side were smashed and the deck ripped open. The stern was awash and she was already sinking. All the lights were out. Captain Burt was cool and resourceful. I got into the third boat that was launched. The ship sank about seven minutes after she was struck." Few boats got away. Thomas Matthews, bosun's mate, saw a sailing vessel at about ten o'clock and in half an hour the dandy-rigged schooner *La Faon* was alongside. The vessel was bound from Swansea for France with coal and picked up twenty-two men from the boats and returned to Swansea to land them. Nine more were found by the American destroyer *Parker* and landed at Pembroke Dock though two of these died at the naval hospital. So just twenty-nine men survived. Ninety-five members of the crew, seven RAMC doctors, eight nurses and forty-three medical orderlies had died. *UC-56*, Kapitanleutnant Wilhelm Kiesewetter commander, had fired the torpedo. The crew of the dandy, Captain Joseph Marie Stephant, mate Louis Marie Dernein, seamen Julien Kersocho and Joseph Marie Raude, and the apprentice Emile Joseph Calloch, were each awarded a silver medal by the Board of Trade.

The *Annie Smith* had been a fishing drifter based at Inverness. She was taken into the navy as a patrol vessel and was sunk in collision on 9 April 1918 near Lundy.

The SS *Plover*, 302 tons, was bound from Portreath for Saundersfoot in ballast when shortly after 1 am on 11 May 1918 the lights of a ship steaming down channel were seen dead ahead. The *Plover*'s helm was put hard to starboard but the Norwegian ship *Lessops* struck her. The *Plover* sank rapidly a few miles north of Lundy. The *Lessops* picked up four men and returned up channel to land them at Cardiff. The ship *Carrowador* picked up the *Plover*'s master Richard Merritt, the mate Arthur Billing, deckhand Robert Williams and chief engineer Charles Kessel who was unconscious. Though the survivors tried artificial respiration on Kessel for three hours they were not able to save him. They were landed at St Ives by the *Carrowador*. The fireman George Langley was believed to have gone down with the wreck.

The schooner *Queen Victoria*, of Poole, was bound from Swansea for Morlaix with patent fuel when becalmed a few miles to the south-east of Lundy on 9 June 1918. A U-boat ordered the crew off and sank the vessel with a scuttling charge. Captain Davey and the three hands got ashore in their boat at Oxwich on the Gower coast.

The trawler *Godrevy*, of Lowestoft, which had rescued the crew of the ketch *Emblem* in January 1916, was now an armed patrol vessel based at Padstow. On 18 May 1918 her gun exploded damaging the deck. Then on the evening of Thursday 20 June 1918 she was twelve miles west-south-west of Lundy when she caught fire and was abandoned by skipper Lockwood and his crew of six who got ashore safely.

The SS *Enfield*, of Newcastle, 2,124 tons gross, which was bound from Barry to St Nazaire with coal, ran ashore on Lundy in thick fog on 4 December 1918. She was towed to Swansea in March 1919 by the tugs *Assistance* and *Lincoln*.

The SS *Marie*, of Bayonne, 1,330 tons, was bound from Penarth to Bordeaux with coal when she was in collision on 18 April 1919 off Lundy with the Swedish steamer *Signe*. The *Marie* was sinking so her crew abandoned and were taken aboard the *Signe* which docked at Cardiff with extensive damage to her bows.

The SS *Canterbury Bell*, of London, 700 tons, left Llanelli with anthracite for Corcubion, Spain, on Wednesday 5 January 1922. A storm struck and the ship's cargo shifted giving her a severe list. The SS *Branstone* rescued the crew and took the *Canterbury Bell* in tow but the vessel sank off Lundy on Thursday afternoon. The *Branstone* landed the crew at Tenby that evening.

The *Madby Ann* was an auxiliary ketch of 100 tons registered at Bideford but owned at Weston-super-Mare. On Saturday 17 June 1928 she was bound from Newport to Courtmacsherry, County Cork, with a cargo of coal and iron sheets. She was seven miles north-west of Lundy late that evening when she developed a leak. Captain Simmonds put back up channel but the water got over the engine and stopped it. Though pumping hard the crew, Sutton and Chapman, failed to overcome the leak so all three abandoned shortly before the ketch sank. At five next morning they were rowing for the coast when William Ward saw them off Lynmouth and towed them ashore with his motorboat.

The SS *Maria Kyriakides*, of Andros, 1,556 tons gross, ran ashore near the granite quarries at 4.20 am on Sunday 25 March 1929. She had been bound from Cardiff to St Malo with coal. Though registered in Greece, the ship was owned by Frank S. Dawson of Cardiff. The master, Antonio Lemonis, two of the engineers and two members of the crew remained aboard and the remaining thirteen men left in Captain F.W. Dark's motorboat *Lerina* for Appledore and returned to Cardiff by train. The cargo was discharged and the ship towed to Ilfracombe. She left there on 9 October 1930 in tow of the tug *King's Cross* and arrived at Grangemouth for repair on 25 October.

The *Maria Kyriakides* ashore near the granite quarries

The SS *Taxiarchis*, of the Greek island of Chios, left Cardiff at 3 pm on Saturday 28 March 1931 bound for Rosario (Argentina) with a cargo of coal and coke. The ship ran ashore at 8 pm and her radio operator, R.J. Lyons, of Ryder Street, Cardiff, was told they were at Bull Point and his distress messages said that. Appledore and Clovelly lifeboats were launched. The master then realised that they were ashore on Lundy so the correct location was signalled. Felix W. Gade, agent to the island's owner, assembled a group to take the life-saving apparatus to the cliff top. The Greek crew remained aboard hoping to get the ship off but at four on Sunday afternoon decided to leave. The first shot put the rocket over the ship and sixteen of the crew were landed by breeches buoy. The master and officers did not leave until Tuesday afternoon when they were also brought up the cliff by breeches buoy. They stayed at the Manor House until taken to Appledore by Captain Dark in the *Lerina*. The vessel was sold to the Coal and Salvage Company and towed to Ilfracombe on 26 July 1933 by the tugs *Eastleigh* and *Westleigh*.

The *Taxiarchis* aground below Halfway Wall

The crew being brought ashore above Halfway Wall Bay

On Friday 6 October 1933 a vessel was seen anchored in a dangerous position in Lundy race. Appledore lifeboat arrived and found that there was no one aboard the former St Ives fishing smack *Mayflower*. Its owner, John Barker, had been a seaman for some years but with the slump in world trade was unemployed and said to be on his way to Bristol to find work. It was believed that Barker had drowned.

The ketch *St Austell*, which was bound from Cardiff to Guernsey with coal, was originally owned at Barnstaple but then at Hull. At about 1 am on Thursday 18 May 1936 she was four miles east-south-east of the south end of Lundy when her auxiliary engine broke down. The vessel was now leaking and at 2.45 the crew burnt hand flares and then fired rockets. The Belfast steamer *Dromara*, Captain G. Montgomery, which had left Port Talbot, then bore down and took the ketch in tow. After two hours the ketch's deck was level with the sea and she was abandoned by her crew, Captain B.J. Brown, mate W.B. Wise and third hand H. Wheelhouse, who got aboard the *Dromara*. Captain Brown's hands had been badly injured. As there was no doctor at Lundy the men were landed at St Ives and Captain Brown taken to hospital. The Trinity House ship *Warden* found the ketch barely afloat and towed it to Swansea.

Thick fog was once again responsible for a ship running ashore. The SS *Carmine Filomena*, 5,253 tons gross, was bound from Swansea with coal for Genoa when she struck Mouse Island a short distance off Rat Island on Lundy's south-eastern point at 9 am on 1 July 1937. Captain Attilo and his crew of twenty-three got ashore. The ship was holed under the bows and the fore-hold flooded. The SS *Ranger* of the Liverpool Salvage Association arrived but the ship could not be got off and was put up for sale by tender. She became a total wreck and her remains still lie there.

SS *Carmine Filomena* ashore at Mouse Island

The motor vessel *Nellie*, 640 tons, struck the Hen and Chickens rocks off Lundy's north-west coast early on the morning of 13 July 1937. She was on passage from Antwerp to Llanelli with scrap iron. Captain Popieul and his crew did their best to save the ship but were forced to abandon in the boats when she went over on to her starboard side. The crew of the *Ranger* which had been attempting to salvage the *Carmine Filomena* responded to the distress signals and picked up the master and nine crew and landed them at Ilfracombe to the cheers of a crowd of holiday makers. The men were then taken to Cardiff where the Belgian consul arranged their return home.

The motor yacht *Freckles* (a former RNLI lifeboat) was owned by Dr J.H. Sewart of Whitchurch, Cardiff, who was secretary of Barry Yacht Club. On the evening of 12 August 1939 Dr Sewart, his wife and their four children were aboard the yacht which anchored near Rat Island. The following morning they raised the anchor but the yacht was swept by the strong tide onto the wreck of the *Carmine Filomena*. F.W. Gade, the island agent, heard the doctor's shouts launched a boat and the family were taken ashore. The yacht broke up.

The Second World War to the 1990s

THE 460 ton SS *Halton*, of Liverpool, struck the Knoll Pins on Lundy's east coast in poor visibility on 27 January 1940. With the pumps failing to cope with the leaking fore-hold, the ship was run ashore on the Landing Beach. The Ilfracombe Salvage Company discharged the cargo of anthracite beans and the *Halton* was towed off by the salvage vessel *Florence*.

The Milford Haven trawler *Kestrel* was fishing to the north of Lundy on 28 March 1941 when attacked by a German aircraft. A bomb exploded close to the vessel damaging it. The crew beached the *Kestrel* on the island and got ashore. Within a few days the rough seas had wrecked the *Kestrel*.

The Dutch motor vessel *Atlas*, of Groningen, was in ballast from Hayle to Newport when she ran aground on the west of the island during the night of 10 October 1942. The mate got ashore but the master and seven members of the crew drowned. A painting of the ship *(right)* hangs in St Helen's church on the island to the memory of Fokko Smit, second engineer of the *Atlas*, and his shipmates.

Convoy EBC 72 was bound from Liverpool to Falmouth. Some of the ships had entered Milford Haven. At 4.54 pm on 14 August 1944 *LST 921* of the US navy was to the south of Lundy when struck on the port side by a torpedo fired by *U-667*, Karl-Heinz Lange commander. The stern of the 1,653 ton ship was torn off and two officers and 41 ratings died. Seventy survivors were picked up by *LST 920* and HMS *Londonderry* and landed at Falmouth. *U-667* sank off La Rochelle on 26 August 1944 having struck a mine – all hands were drowned.

At 2.15 am on Sunday 18 July 1948 the 395 ton motor-vessel *Amstelstroom*, of Amsterdam, bound for Newport with a general cargo, ran ashore in thick fog at Battery Point on Lundy's west coast. The vessel's lifeboat was lost so the mate Nicholas Stolp went over the side and attempted to swim ashore with a line. He failed and his mates pulled him back aboard. At daylight they were able to swing one of the derricks against the cliff and climb to the top. Four of the crew, two of whom were badly bruised, were taken ashore by Appledore lifeboat the following day. The master, Wessel Jansen, and the other six members of the crew stayed at Lundy hoping to assist in salvaging the ship. Within a couple of days however the vessel was beyond salvage.

On the morning of 13 November 1949 the SS *Monte Gurugu*, of Bilbao, 3,554 tons, which was bound from Newport to Genoa with coal, ran into a heavy north-west gale as it steamed to pass south of Lundy. The ship was soon taking on water through her damaged bows. Her fore-hold was flooded and when Captain Luis Bilbao-Munairz attempted to turn back up channel he found that the ship would not answer the helm and concluded that the rudder was damaged. Soon after the radio operator had made the SOS call the decision was made to abandon ship. The two lifeboats and a dinghy left the ship. One of the lifeboats capsized throwing a dozen men into the sea. Three lifeboat stations were alerted. The Clovelly lifeboat set off first but was given an incorrect position and initially searched to the south of Hartland Point. The Appledore lifeboat left her moorings at 6.45 am and two hours later found the capsized boat which was empty. Shortly afterwards the crew found one man in the sea and five bodies. It went straight to Ilfracombe and landed the man who was taken to hospital. The Ilfracombe lifeboat was launched at 7.18 and made for Woolacombe Bay. Just after 9.00 the ship's other boat was seen being driven towards the shore by the gale. The Ilfracombe lifeboat got a line aboard and towed it away from the breakers and took twenty-three men aboard. They were landed at Ilfracombe at 10.30. The ship's dinghy drove ashore at the southern end of Woolacombe Bay. Men on the shore waded out and got the ship's radio operator, Juan Lozano Rico, ashore and took him to the Grey House at Vention from where he was taken to hospital. The other man in the dinghy could not be saved. The search continued but no more survivors were found. A total of twelve men had drowned. Five were not found and seven were buried at Marlborough Cemetery, Ilfracombe. The crews of the three lifeboats all received awards from Spain. The Royal National Lifeboat Institution awarded coxswain Cecil Irwin, of the Ilfracombe lifeboat, its silver medal for gallantry, a second service bar to his bronze medal to Sydney Cann, coxswain of the Appledore lifeboat, and increased monetary awards to the coxswain and crew at Clovelly.

The tug *Jaunty* was towing the tank landing craft *LCT 7009* from the Clyde to Sheerness. On the evening of 19 August 1951 the plates of the craft began to open, the sea flooded in, and she capsized. The *Jaunty* slipped the tow.

On 2 May 1954 the *LCT 565* parted its tow from the tug *Thunderer* in a gale. The vessel was found on the rocks about a quarter of a mile north of the Old Light by F.W. Gade. It was a total wreck.

A few lines from the author's diary kept when living at Mumbles: "Wednesday 22 January 1975. The rain still going strong this morning. A fresh SW gale behind it. The Panamanian registered *Robert* sank off Lundy. Cardiff to Rouen with coal she developed a list near Lundy and got into the anchorage. The crew were taken off by the 70ft lifeboat stationed off Clovelly. Tugs could not get out to her. The list increased this morning and she sank in the anchorage. This will probably prove a hazard to vessels seeking shelter in future." The lifeboat *Charles H. Barrett (Civil Service No. 35)* was at anchor in Lundy roads on Tuesday 21 January when her crew saw the motor vessel *Robert* arrive with a strong list to starboard. The lifeboat launched her

The lifeboat *Charles H. Barrett* stands by the listing motor vessel *Robert*

inflatable boat and took off the crew of four after they had anchored the vessel. A strong gale was blowing from the west and the sea was rough under the lee of the island. That evening the lifeboat moved closer to the island and transferred three of the *Robert*'s crew to the motor-vessel *Polar Bear*, Lundy's supply ship, which landed them at Ilfracombe. The vessel's master remained aboard the lifeboat. By the following morning the list had increased to 70 degrees and the ship sank at 11.40 a little over a mile from the South Light and half a mile from Tibbetts Point. The lifeboat landed the master at Ilfracombe that afternoon.

On the morning of 31 May 1975 the crew of a Nimrod aircraft reported seeing a red flare about twenty miles to the west of Lundy. A Whirlwind helicopter from RAF Chivenor picked up the five crew of the trawler *Noordzee*, of Ostend, who had taken to the life-raft as the vessel sank.

In the early hours of 6 November 1980 the coastguard station at Mumbles received a distress message from the 480 ton MV *Kaaksburg*, of Itzehoe near Hamburg, that her engine had failed. A near gale force wind from the north-east was driving the vessel, which was in ballast from Sharpness to Kiel, towards Lundy. A Sea-King helicopter from Brawdy, Pembrokeshire, arrived over the island at 4 am to find the ship ashore north of the granite quarries. Lights were seen on the cliff so the pilot Flt Lt Peter Wallace landed on the cliff top and winchman Sgt Griffiths went down to lead the crew to safety. All seven, including the female cook Elke Wollert, were flown to Chivenor where they changed into dry clothes and enjoyed an RAF breakfast. The vessel became a total wreck.

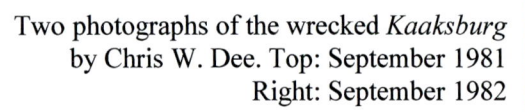

Two photographs of the wrecked *Kaaksburg* by Chris W. Dee. Top: September 1981 Right: September 1982

At 7.30 on the evening of 3 March 1993 the crew of the trawler *Charlynnell*, of Newquay, Cornwall, realised she was leaking badly and decided to run for Lundy. Their Mayday message resulted in a Sea-King helicopter from Brawdy, which was on a night-time training exercise off St Ann's Head, Pembrokeshire, being diverted to the scene. The pilot Flt Lt Alan Coy, reported that as they arrived the vessel was sinking and her three crew had jumped into the sea. The helicopter crew rescued them from the icy water and flew them to hospital in Barnstaple.

In September 1995 a group of friends from Monmouthshire were on a yachting holiday and had called in at Lundy where they anchored the yacht to go ashore. As they returned to the beach they realised that the anchor cable had parted and the yacht was heading towards the rocks. The owner Peter Walton dived in and attempted to swim to the yacht. Barrie Portsmith, of the Old Swan, Abercarn, saw that Walton was in danger of drowning so dived in and brought him ashore. The yacht broke up on striking the rocks.

At 10.30 on the evening of 7 November 1995 the emergency services were alerted when a signal was received from an automatic distress beacon. The signal was from the beam trawler *Provider Two*, of Falmouth, but worked out of Newlyn. A number of trawlers and lifeboats searched to the north-west of Lundy but were not able to locate the vessel. Eventually a helicopter found a life-raft and a patch of diesel fuel. The vessel had sunk with its crew; skipper Peter Smith and brothers Tim and Paul Bennett drowned.

There are fortunately fewer wrecks on and around Lundy now than at any time in recorded history. This is thanks to, firstly, the work of Trinity House (p.10) in establishing and maintaining lighthouses and other navigational aids; secondly, the move from sail to steam and motor engines, giving ships greater power and manoeuvrability; thirdly, legislation governing the safety of vessels, for example the campaign by Samuel Plimsoll M.P. which resulted in load lines being compulsory on ships to prevent overloading (Merchant Shipping Act 1876). Then came the development of radio (early twentieth century) which enabled vessels to request aid and others to respond; and most recently radar (developed during and after World War II) and satellite navigation (1990s) which permit safe navigation in fog and allow a ship's crew to know their position at all times. The decline in coal and metal exports has also greatly reduced the number of ships in the Bristol Channel passing Lundy, only partially offset by a few very large vessels delivering car imports to Royal Portbury Dock, Bristol.

Bibliography and sources

As I pointed out in the Introduction these articles and books contain many inaccuracies as to the name, circumstance or date of a wreck:
Lundy Shipwrecks Michael Bouquet (Lundy Field Society Annual Reports of 1967 and 1969)
Lundy A. and M. Langham (David and Charles, 1970)
The Island of Lundy A.F. Langham (Alan Sutton, 1994)
Shipwreck Index of the British Isles Volume 1 R. & B. Larn (Lloyd's Register of Shipping, 1995)
Light over Lundy Myrtle Ternstrom (Whittles Publishing, 2007)
Lundy Island: pirates, plunder and shipwreck Brian French (Grosvenor House, 2011)

The sources I used:
Lloyd's List, Lloyd's Register of Shipping, Shipping and Mercantile Gazette, Bristol Mercury, Bristol Mirror, Felix Farley's Bristol Journal, The Cambrian (published in Swansea), *Cardiff Times, Cheltenham Chronicle, Evening Express* (published in Cardiff), *Exeter & Plymouth Gazette, Lakes Falmouth Packet & Cornwall Advertiser, Glasgow Herald, Monmouthshire Merlin, North Devon Journal, Pembrokeshire Herald, South Wales Daily News, Western Daily Mercury, Western Daily Press, Western Gazette, Western Morning News, West Somerset Free Press, Western Mail* (published in Cardiff).

Most of these publications are now available online at:
British Newspaper Archive (by subscription)
Welsh Newspapers Online (at present this site only covers the years up to 1919)

Information on the German submarines was derived from uboat.net

Index of names of ships

A Daughter's Offering	54
Abbotsford	15
Admiral	32
Adolphe	31
Advance	54
Agricola	70
Alarm	38, 42
Albion	18, 33, 34
Albrecht	45
Alert	17, 24
Alexandria	70
Alphonse	31
Amazon	44
Amstelstroom	76
Ann	16, 18
Ann & Mary	14
Anne Williams	30
Annie Smith	72
Apphia	33
Archelaus	19
Argo	34
Argus	17
Ariel	20
Arndale	67
Arosa	67
Arturo	42
Ashdale	52
Ashley	17
Assistance	72
Asterias	35, 36
Athlet	44
Atlas	76
Augoustis	67
Auricula	66
Auspicious	20
Avon	20
Baines Hawkins	46
Ballydoon	58
Baltic	7
Balvenie	69
Bath City	60, 61
Bay Fisher	52
Bayano	68
Belinda	34
Ben McCree	24
Ben Strome	71
Benamain	52
Beryl	36
Bessie Mitchell	35
Bessie Stephens	71
Betsey	37
Bicton	30
Boileau	54
Boswedden	48
Bottreaux Castle	23
Boucan	49, 51
Bowesfield	46
Branstone	72
Brenda	36, 37
Breiz Huel	67
Brilliant Star	48
Britannia	19
Briton	47
Brothers	30
Burnswark	45
C.S. Atkinson	61
Cam	57
Cambronne	43, 45
Canada	38
Canterbury Bell	72
Carmine Filomena	75
Carnalea	71
Caroline	32
Carrowador	72
Castillian	67
Catherine	19
Catherine Hendry	59
Catherine Sutton	55
Catherine Thomas	23
Cereda	66
Charles	22
Charles Goddard	43
Charles H. Barrett	77
Charles W. Anderson	54
Charlynnell	79
Chesapeake	24
Chilgrove	7
Choice	22
Chrysolite	54
City of Exeter	3, 50
City of Gloucester	51
Clara	18
Clarissa	60
Clipper	55
Clutha River	69
Coila	55
Columba	31
Comus	13
Concord	7
Corinthian	24
Cornwall	36
Cottingham	69
Countess of Bective	19
Courage	70
Crescent	17
D. Roma	59
Dandy	35
Daniel	7
Devonia	69
Diamond	33, 57
Diligent	23
Dove	8
Dovey Belle	66
Drayton	60

Dromara 74	Fleece 7	Henry Southam 36
Eagle 60	Florence 61, 76	Hercules 61
Earl of Jersey 59	Flying Fox 48, 49	Hermina 33
East Anglian 32	Flying Scotsman 51	Heroine 45
Eastleigh 73	Flying Serpent 61	Highgate 52
Éclair 24	Flying Swallow 51	Hilversum 70
Edward Arthur 69	Forest Belle 55	Himalaya 36, 37
Eidswold 27	Four Friends 17	Hirondelle 47
Electric 50, 51	Foy 66	Hope 14, 21, 24, 25
Eliza 17, 19, 35, 37, 38	Frances Anne 14	Hopewell 7
Eliza Jones 52	Freckles 75	Hornet 46
Elizabeth 16	Frederick 22	Hoy Head 47
Elizabeth & Ann 15	Friendship 67	Hungate 61
Elliot and Jeffrey 57	Galloper 49	I.O 14
Elsie 49	Gannet 50, 55, 59	Infanta 58
Emblem 69, 72	Gazelle 70	Ingoldsby 45
Emily 39, 56	Gironde 45	Inversnaid 48
Emma 44, 68	Giuseppina Ilardi 61	Iona/Iona II 3, 26, 27, 65
Empress 43	Gladiolus 52	Irene 52
Empress of India 49	Glenart Castle 71	Ismyr 54
Enfield 72	Glenbervie 49	J.C.A. 32
Erin 15	Glenlyon 19	J.E.S.S. 66
Escort 60	Glenmavis 49	James 21, 24
Estrella de Mar 8	Godrevy 69, 72	James & Agnes 66
Ethel 3, 41, 42	Gold Digger 39	Jane 23
Eurydice 46	Gower 17	Jaunty 77
Expedient 19	Gratitude 67	Jeanne et Robert 39
Expedition 18	Guiding Star 59	Jenny 7
Experiment 18	Gurley 70	Jessie 59
Experimenter 18	Gwydir Castle 32	Jeune Charles 54
Express 33, 49	H.R. Tilton 42	Jeune Emma 14
Faders Minde 15	Halton 76	John & Mary 16
Falcon 47, 53, 54	Hannah More 3, 30	Joseph R. Folsom 21
Fame 13	Harmony 18	Juanita 48, 49
Fanny 39	Harpy 9	Julia 33
Far West 29	Harvest Queen 66	Kaaksburg 5, 78
Fatfield 53	Haxby 66	Kaisow 60
Favourite 54	Hector 7, 30	Kate 18, 56
Fear Not 59	Helen 29	Keldhead 38
Fiona 61	Heligan 43	Kestrel 76
Fish Girl 60	Henry 48, 49	King's Cross 73

Kingsley 61	Maria Kyriakides 73	P.C. Petersen 59
Kingston 16	Marie 7, 72	Pallion 39
Knatten 70	Mariner 17	Panaja Eleusa 19
Kong Sverre 21	Marion 45	Paola Revello 44
La Faon 71	Mary 17, 36	Parker 72
Lady Clive 32, 33	Mary Ann 18, 19, 24, 38, 47	Paul Paix 71
Lady Lewis 60	Mary Anne 39	Peace 23
Lady Louise 43	Mary Ashburner 67	Peer of the Realm 47
Lamb 13	Mary Isabella 18	Pelaw 42, 45
Langley 43	Mary Maria 29	Pembridge 53
Lanisley 55	Mary Orr 69	Pilot 16
Lark 71	Matilda 3, 26, 27, 28	Plover 61, 72
LCT 565 77	Mayflower 74	Plymouth 22
LCT 7009 77	Millicent 58	Polar Bear 78
Leda 37	Minna 44	Polly 7
Léocadie 22	Molly 68	Port Darwin 59
Lerina 73	Montagu 3, 62, 63, 64, 65	Prairie Flower 51
Lessops 72	Monte Gurugu 76	Pride of the Taff 42
Levant 47	Morrison 13	Providence 34, 39
Lewis Charles 23	Mount Park 70	Provider Two 79
Lincoln 72	Myrtle Tree 7	Prudential 59
Linda Grace 67	Mystery 57	Queen of Peace 31
Little Racer 46	Nancy & Betsey 7	Queen Victoria 72
Llandovery Castle 71	Nautilus 33	Quicksilver 16
Loire 22	Navarino 18	Racine 67
Londonderry 76	Nellie 75	Radnor 51
Lord Oriel 18	Neptune 17	Rajah 3, 57
Louisa 19	New Prosperous 49	Ralph Creyke 43, 45
Louise 19	Noord 47	Ranger 22, 24, 75
LST 920 76	Noordzee 78	Rapid 15
LST 921 76	Norah 52	Rattler 44, 51
Lubentia 35	Norseman 55	Red Rose 57
Lundy Puffin 64	Odin 17	Refuge 42
Madby Ann 72	Ohr 60	Rewa 71
Maid of Erin 19	Oliphant 7	Richard 33
Mandalay 59	Orange Branch 20	Rival 52
Mandamus 19	Orion 34	Riviere 16
Marco Polo 44	Orne 67	Robert 65, 77, 78
Margaret 34	Oscar 31	Robert & Mary 15
Margaret Hain 69	Ostendais 15	Robert Brown 70
Maria 55	Ostrich 37, 38	Rochdale 17

Rosario 49	Success 36	Vagliano Brothers 47
Rose 18	Susan 17	Valentine 23
Rover 8, 58	Susan Gibbs 45	Valiant 19
Royal Briton 58, 59	Susanna 7	Vendome 48
Rupee 70	Swift 33, 42	Venedocian 66
St Austell 74	Sylphiden 18	Venus 14
St Austell Packet 18	Syntra 52	Ver 34, 35
Salado 57, 58	T.G.V. 29	Victoria 58
Salisbury 54	Tagona 69	Victory 19
Sally 18	Tartar 24	Village Belle 39
Sambo 69	Taxiarchis 68, 73, 74	Vine 9
Sandhurst 66	Tempus 67	Vixen 31
Sandwich Bay 29	Tertius 27	Volage 35
Sarah 17	Thistlemor 66, 67	Volusia 23
Sarah Ann 50	Thomas & Ann 13	W.A. Brown 24
Screamer 24	Thomas Collingdon 49	Wanderer 41
Sea Prince 53, 54, 61	Thomas Varcoe 36	Warden 74
Secret 54	Thunderer 77	Warwick 7
Sedgemoor 37	Tintern Abbey 68	Waterwitch 19
Shannon 27	Tre Søstre 56	Wave 36
Signe 72	Trelissick 32	Wesleyan 24
Sinope 23	Trevose 45	Wesleyana 22
Sir Bevis 38	Trident 22	West Dock 32
Skart 61	Tromp 67	Westleigh 73
Soar 69	True Blue 23, 39	Westward 59
Somerset 7	Tunisie 53	Why Not 25
South Australian 51, 65	Tweed 44	G.N. Wilkinson 43
Sovereign 52	Tweedsdale 51	William 25
Sparfield 33	Tyne 61	William Banks 47
Speculation 14	U-19 70	Wimbledon 46
Speedwell 34	U-24 69	Winnie 66
Spitfire 59, 66	U-55 71	Wizard 19
Spray 51	U-57 70	Woodman 17
Springbok 57	U-86 71	Wye 7
Springwell 57	U-96 70	Young Clifford 70
St Austell 74	U-667 76	Zenith 55
Star 60	UC-2 69	Zoodochos Pighi 45
Start 39	UC-51 70	
Storjohann 45	UC-56 72	
Storm Nymph 34, 35	UC-77 70	
Stranger 31	Unity 9, 15, 16	